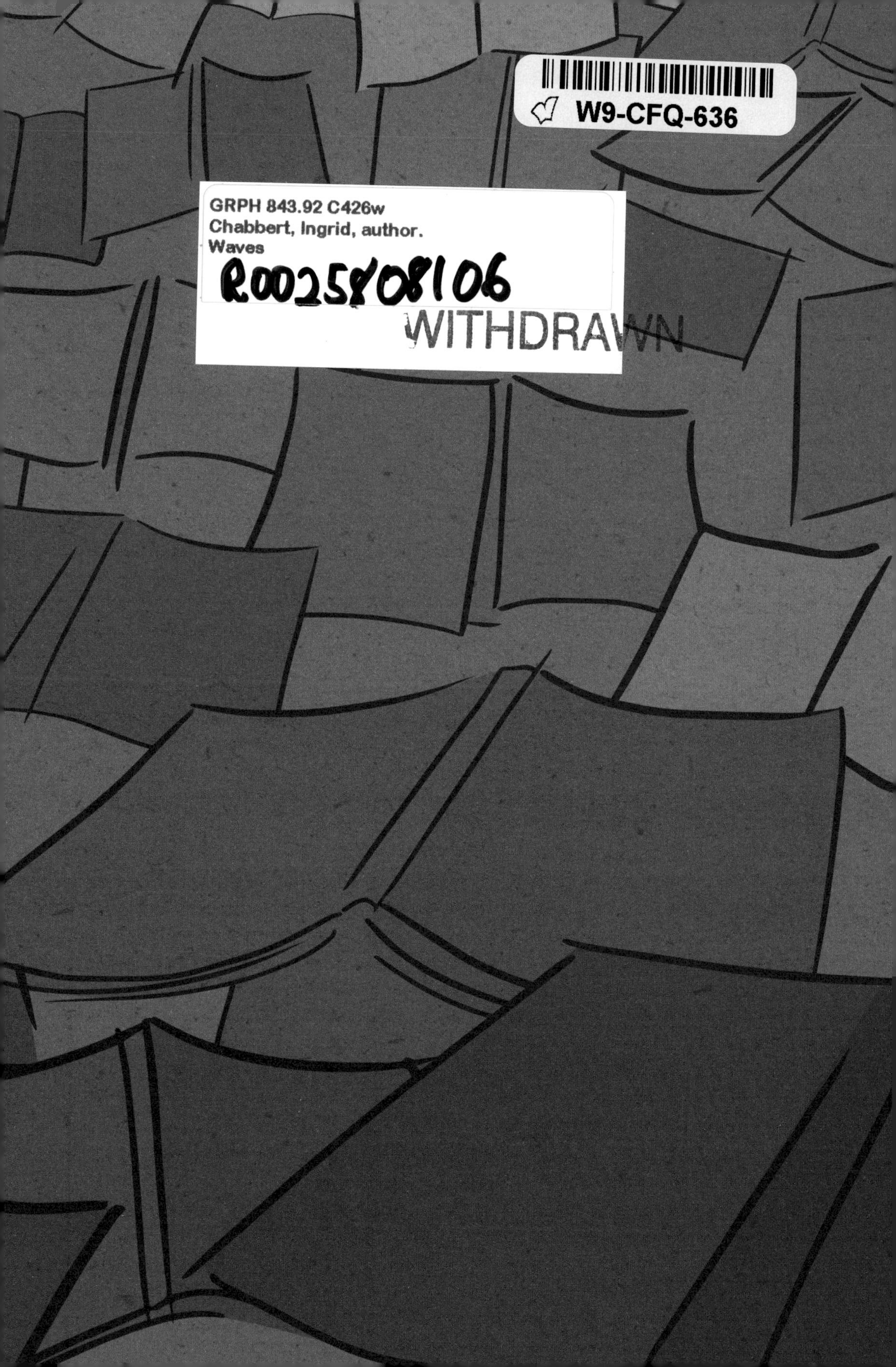

WAVES ™

Published by
ARCHAIA ™

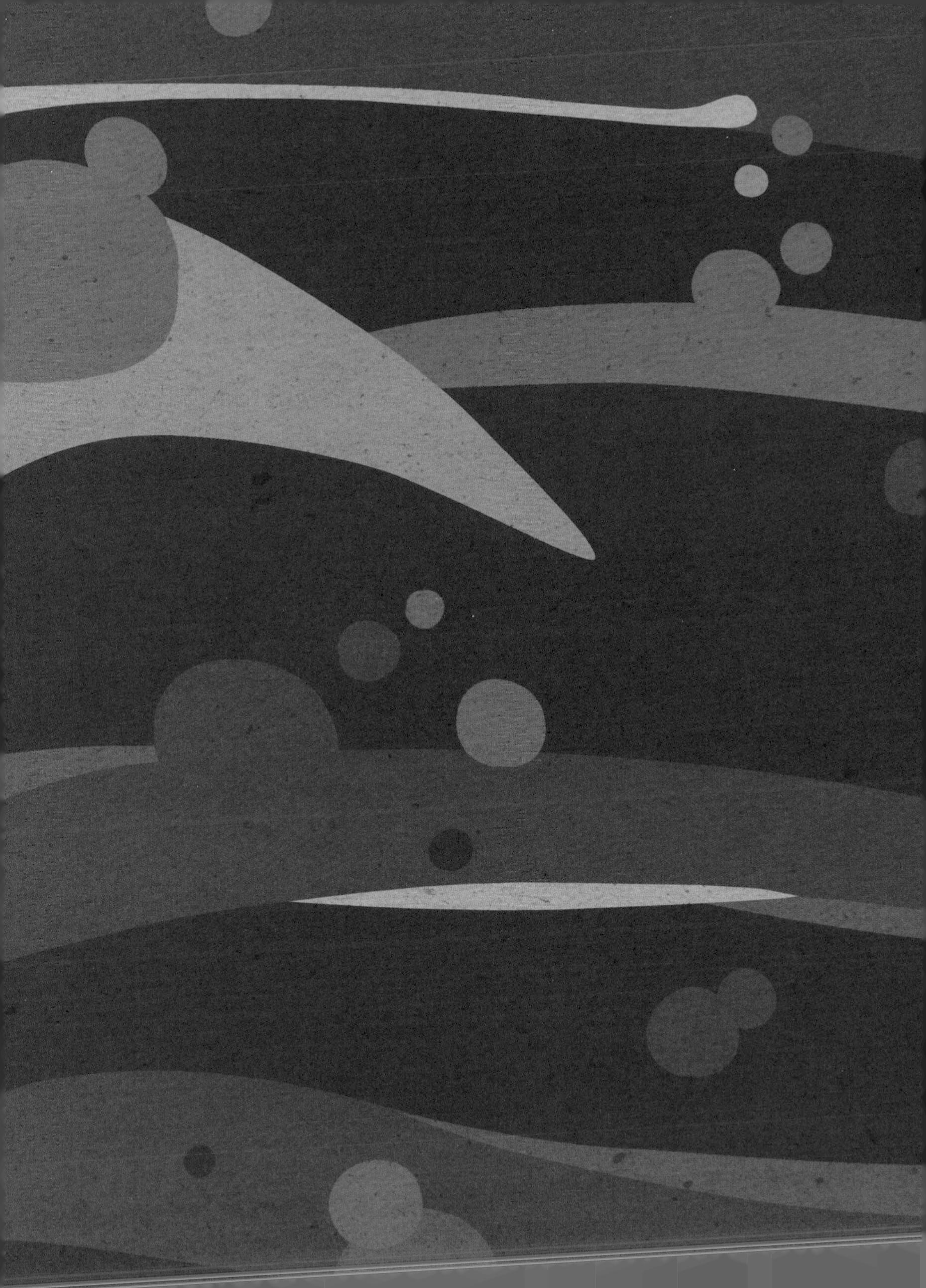

WAVES ™

WRITTEN BY **INGRID CHABBERT**

ILLUSTRATED BY **CAROLE MAUREL**

TRANSLATED BY **EDWARD GAUVIN**

LETTERED BY **DERON BENNETT**

ARCHAIA • LOS ANGELES, CALIFORNIA

COVER BY **CAROLE MAUREL**

ENGLISH EDITION
DESIGNER **JILLIAN CRAB**
EDITOR **SIERRA HAHN**

Ross Richie CEO & Founder
Joy Huffman CFO
Matt Gagnon Editor-in-Chief
Filip Sablik President, Publishing & Marketing
Stephen Christy President, Development
Lance Kreiter Vice President, Licensing & Merchandising
Phil Barbaro Vice President, Finance & Human Resources
Arune Singh Vice President, Marketing
Bryce Carlson Vice President, Editorial & Creative Strategy
Scott Newman Manager, Production Design
Kate Henning Manager, Operations
Spencer Simpson Manager, Sales
Sierra Hahn Executive Editor
Jeanine Schaefer Executive Editor
Dafna Pleban Senior Editor
Shannon Watters Senior Editor
Eric Harburn Senior Editor
Whitney Leopard Editor
Cameron Chittock Editor
Chris Rosa Editor
Matthew Levine Editor

Sophie Philips-Roberts Assistant Editor
Gavin Gronenthal Assistant Editor
Michael Moccio Assistant Editor
Amanda LaFranco Executive Assistant
Jillian Crab Design Coordinator
Michelle Ankley Design Coordinator
Kara Leopard Production Designer
Marie Krupina Production Designer
Grace Park Production Design Assistant
Chelsea Roberts Production Design Assistant
Samantha Knapp Production Design Assistant
Elizabeth Loughridge Accounting Coordinator
Stephanie Hocutt Social Media Coordinator
José Meza Event Coordinator
Holly Aitchison Operations Coordinator
Megan Christopher Operations Assistant
Rodrigo Hernandez Mailroom Assistant
Morgan Perry Direct Market Representative
Cat O'Grady Marketing Assistant
Breanna Sarpy Executive Assistant

WAVES, May 2019. Published by Archaia, a division of Boom Entertainment, Inc. Waves is ™ and © 2017 Steinkis. All rights reserved. Archaia™ and the Archaia logo are trademarks of Boom Entertainment, Inc., registered in various countries and categories. All characters, events, and institutions depicted herein are fictional. Any similarity between any of the names, characters, persons, events, and/or institutions in this publication to actual names, characters, and persons, whether living or dead, events, and/or institutions is unintended and purely coincidental.

Originally published in French by Steinkis as *Sourdes.*

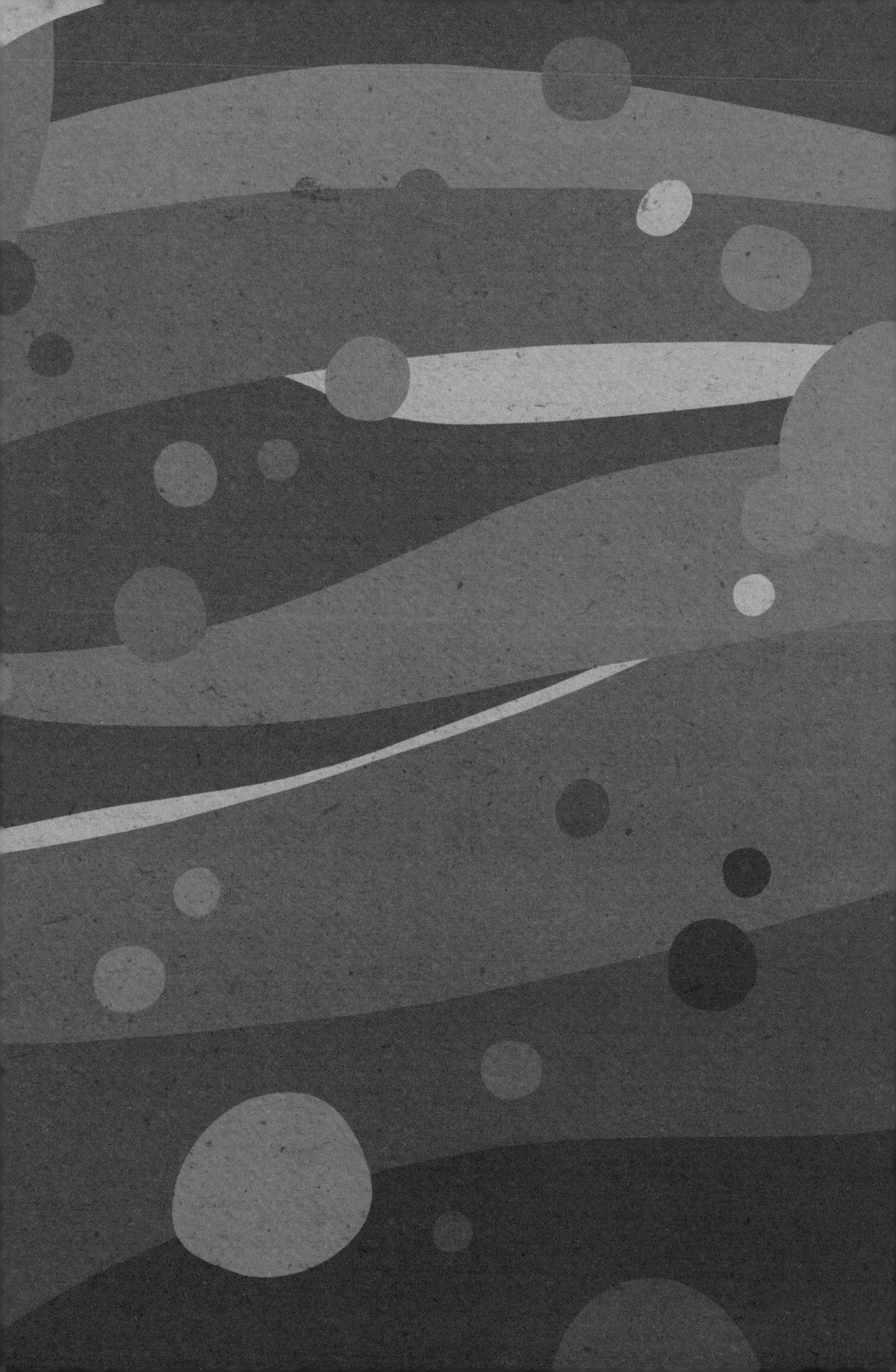

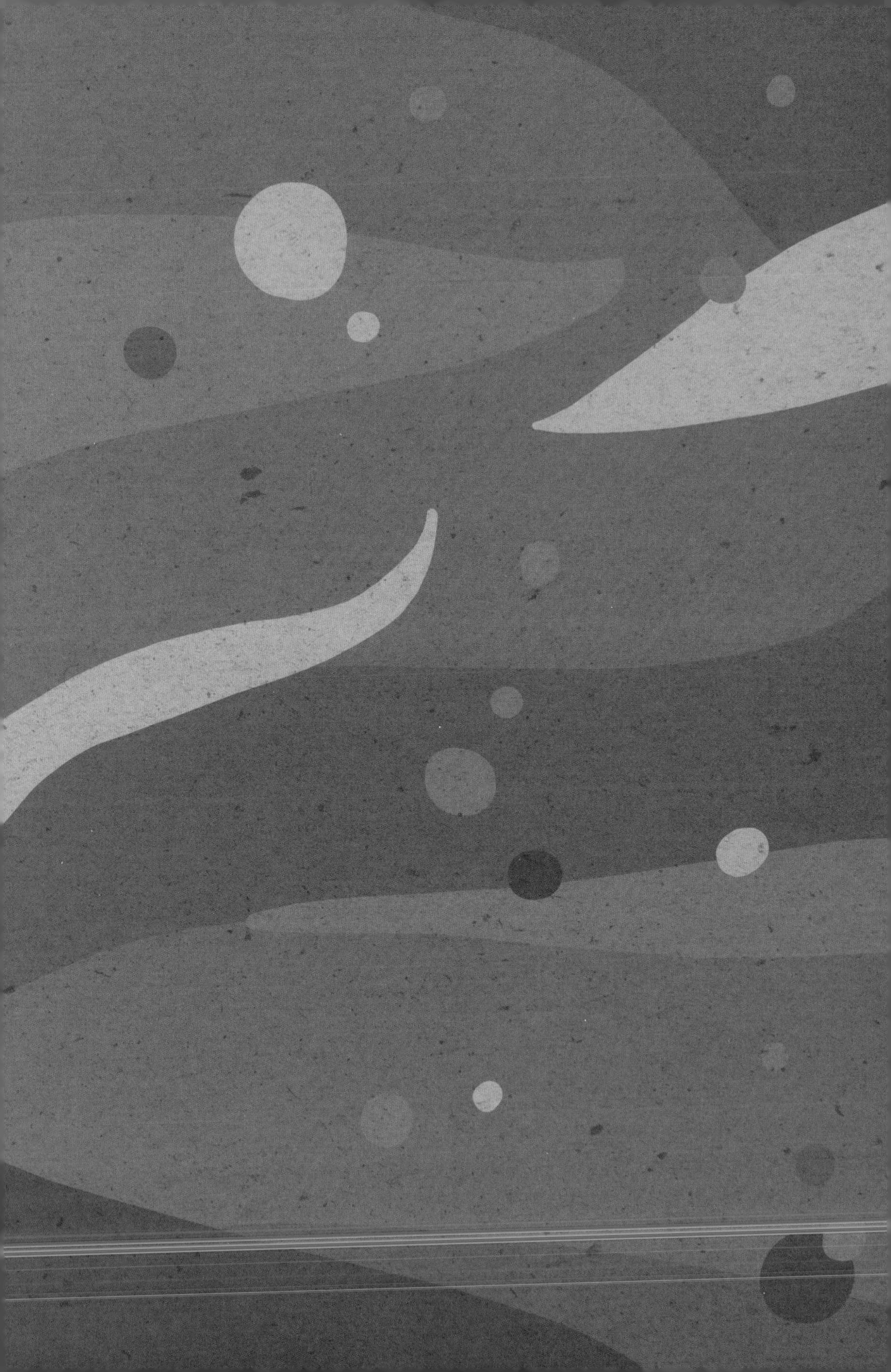

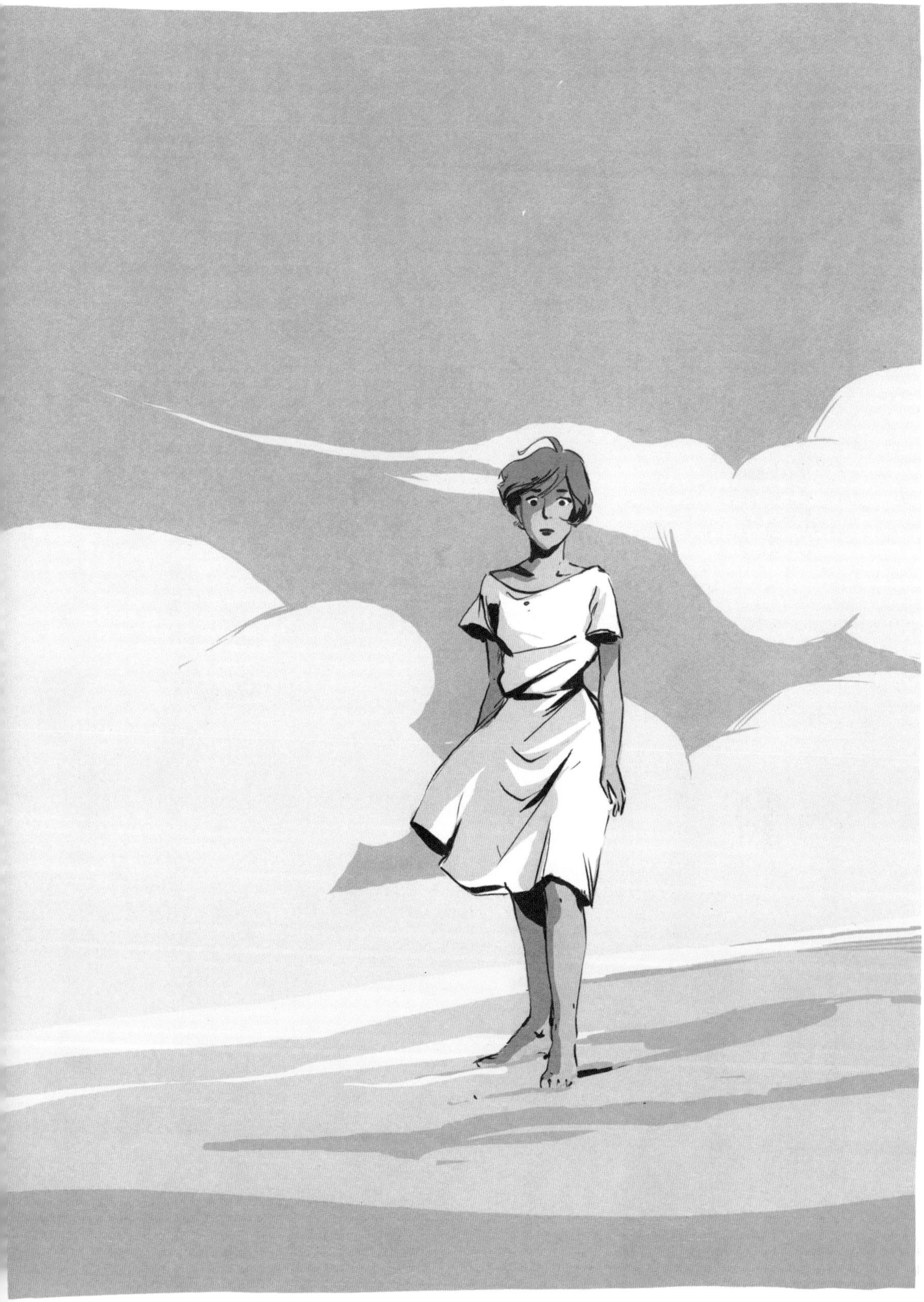

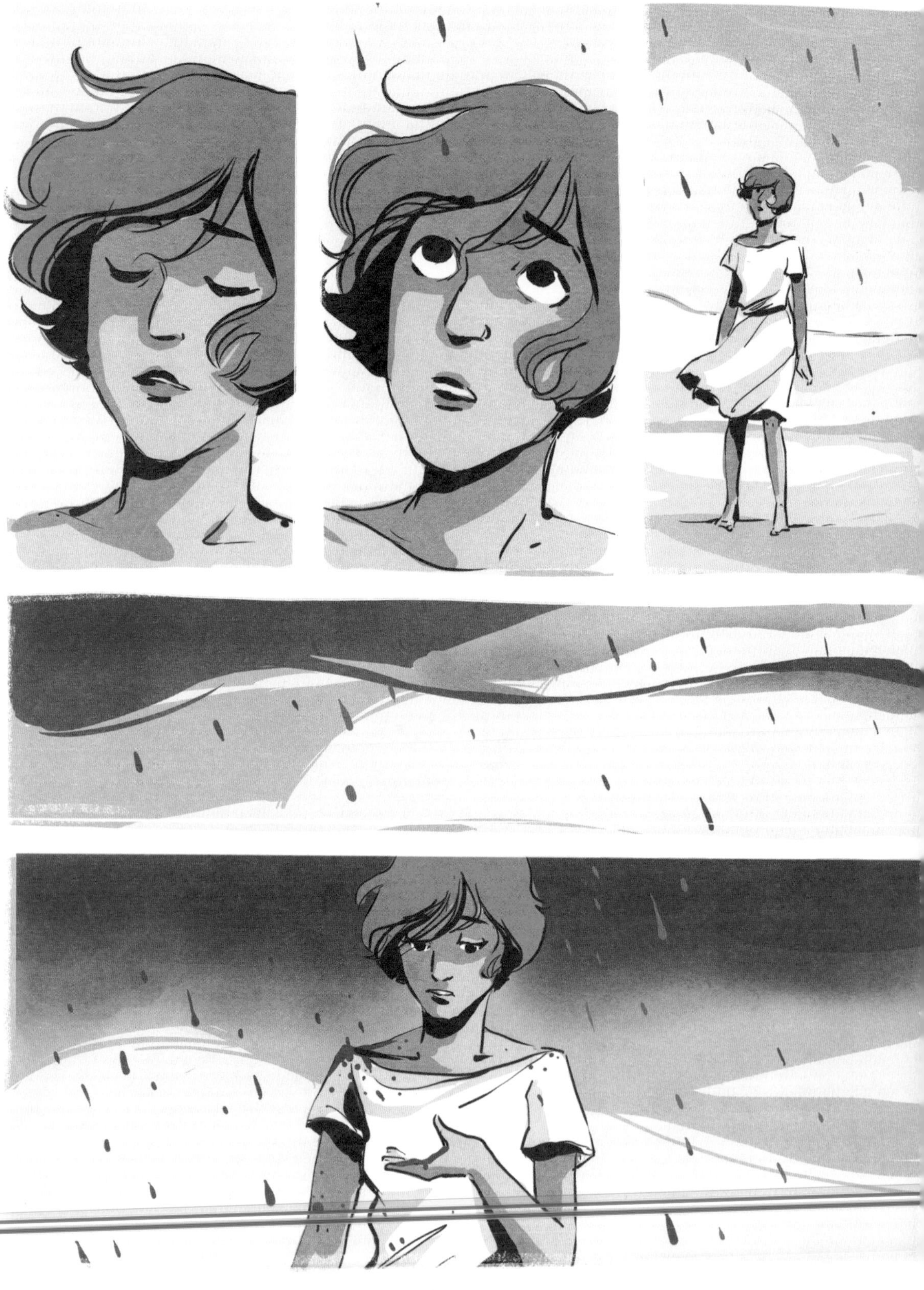

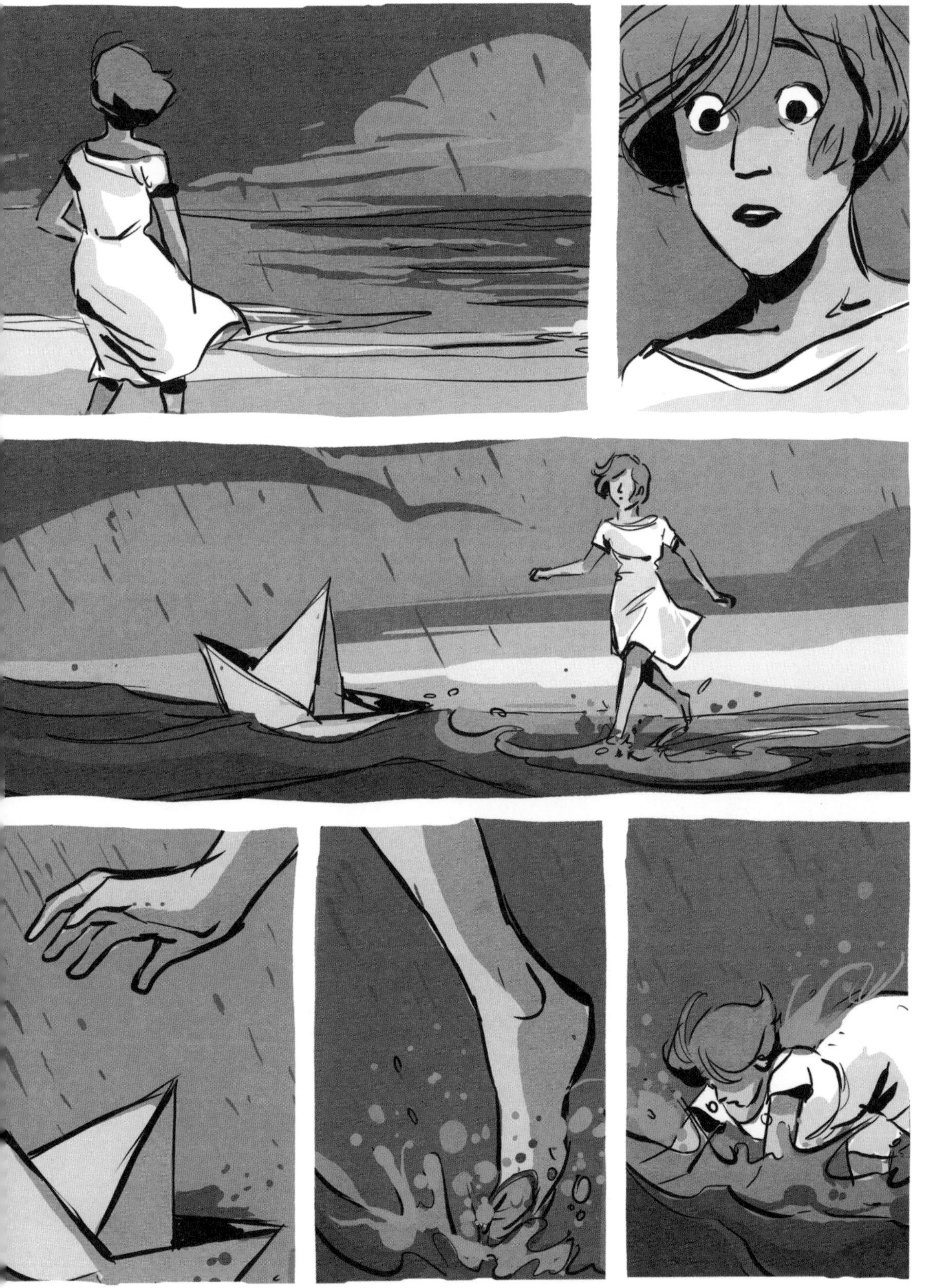

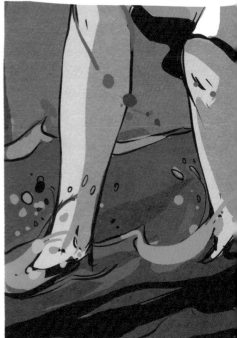

SOMETIMES WE DROWN, DRINKING IN THE SEA.

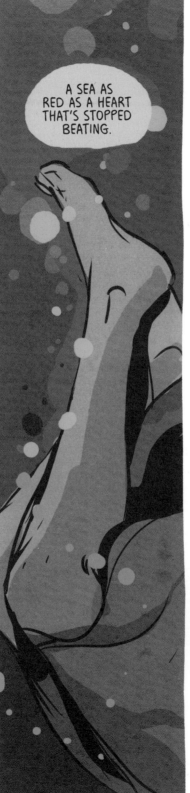

A SEA AS RED AS A HEART THAT'S STOPPED BEATING.

WE LOOK UP, FROM AN UNDERWATER CROSSROADS -- RETURN TO THE SURFACE OR LET GO.

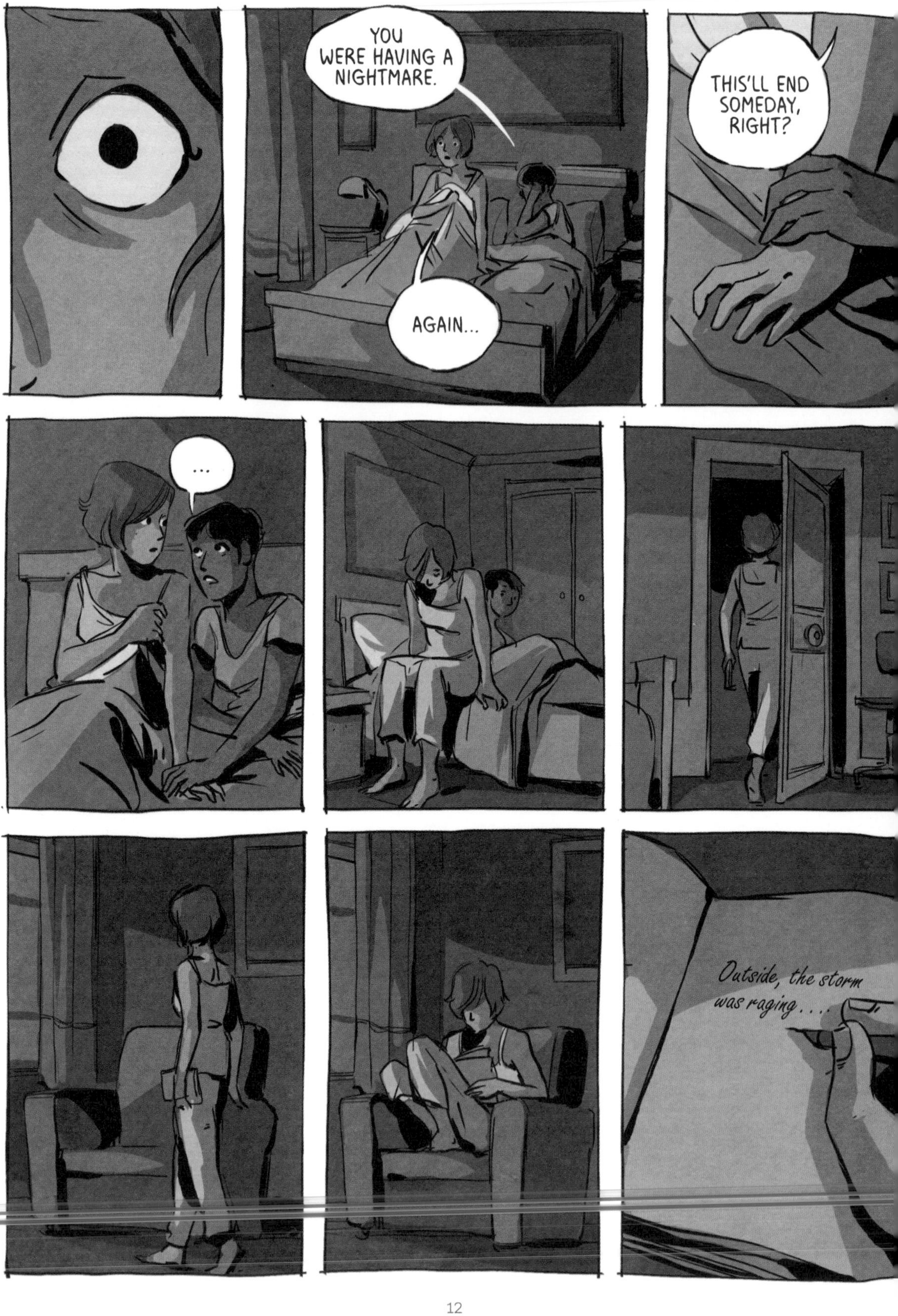
YOU WERE HAVING A NIGHTMARE.
AGAIN...
THIS'LL END SOMEDAY, RIGHT?
...
Outside, the storm was raging....

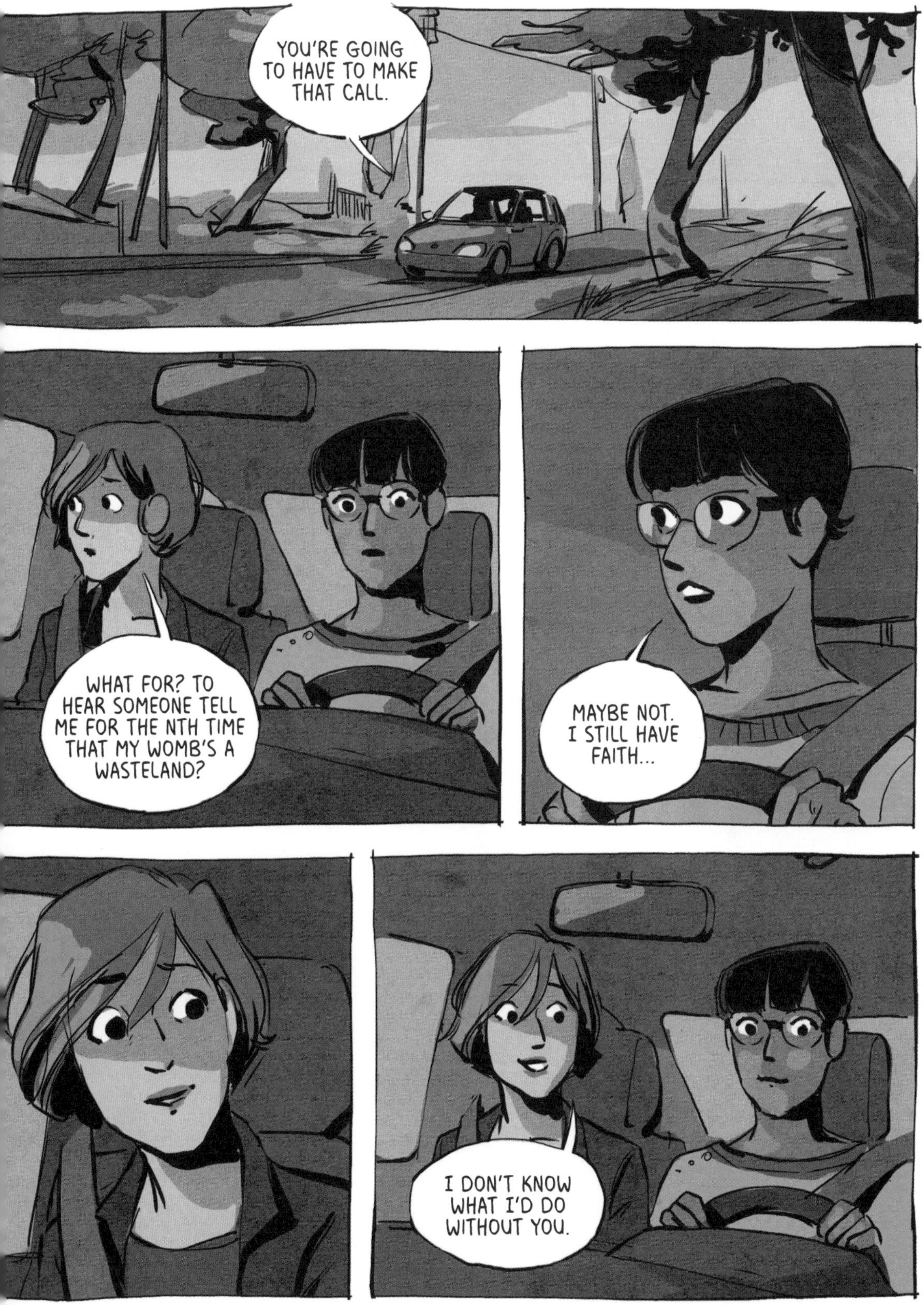

YOU'RE GOING TO HAVE TO MAKE THAT CALL.
WHAT FOR? TO HEAR SOMEONE TELL ME FOR THE NTH TIME THAT MY WOMB'S A WASTELAND?
MAYBE NOT. I STILL HAVE FAITH...
I DON'T KNOW WHAT I'D DO WITHOUT YOU.

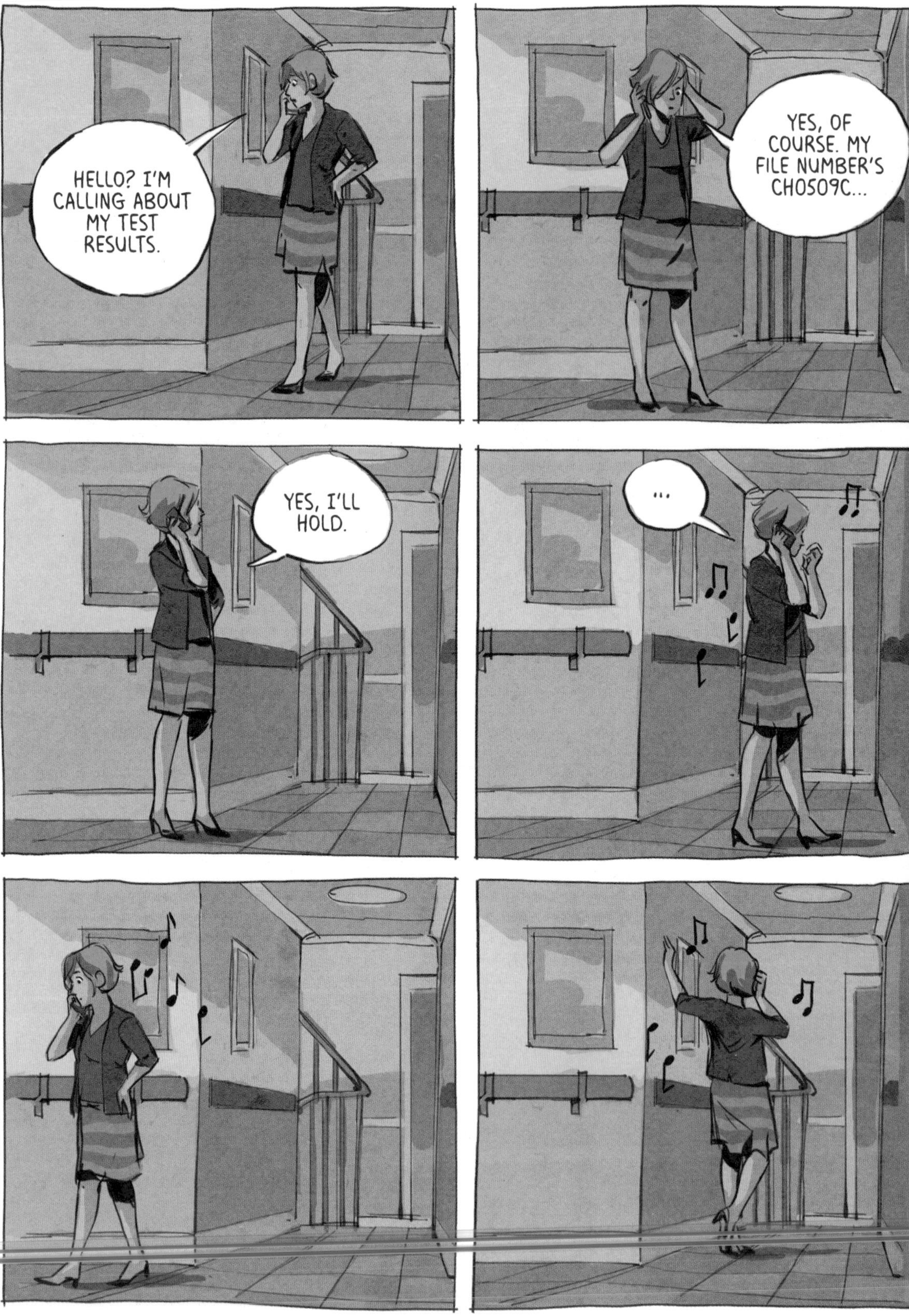
HELLO? I'M CALLING ABOUT MY TEST RESULTS.
YES, OF COURSE. MY FILE NUMBER'S CH0509C...
YES, I'LL HOLD.
...

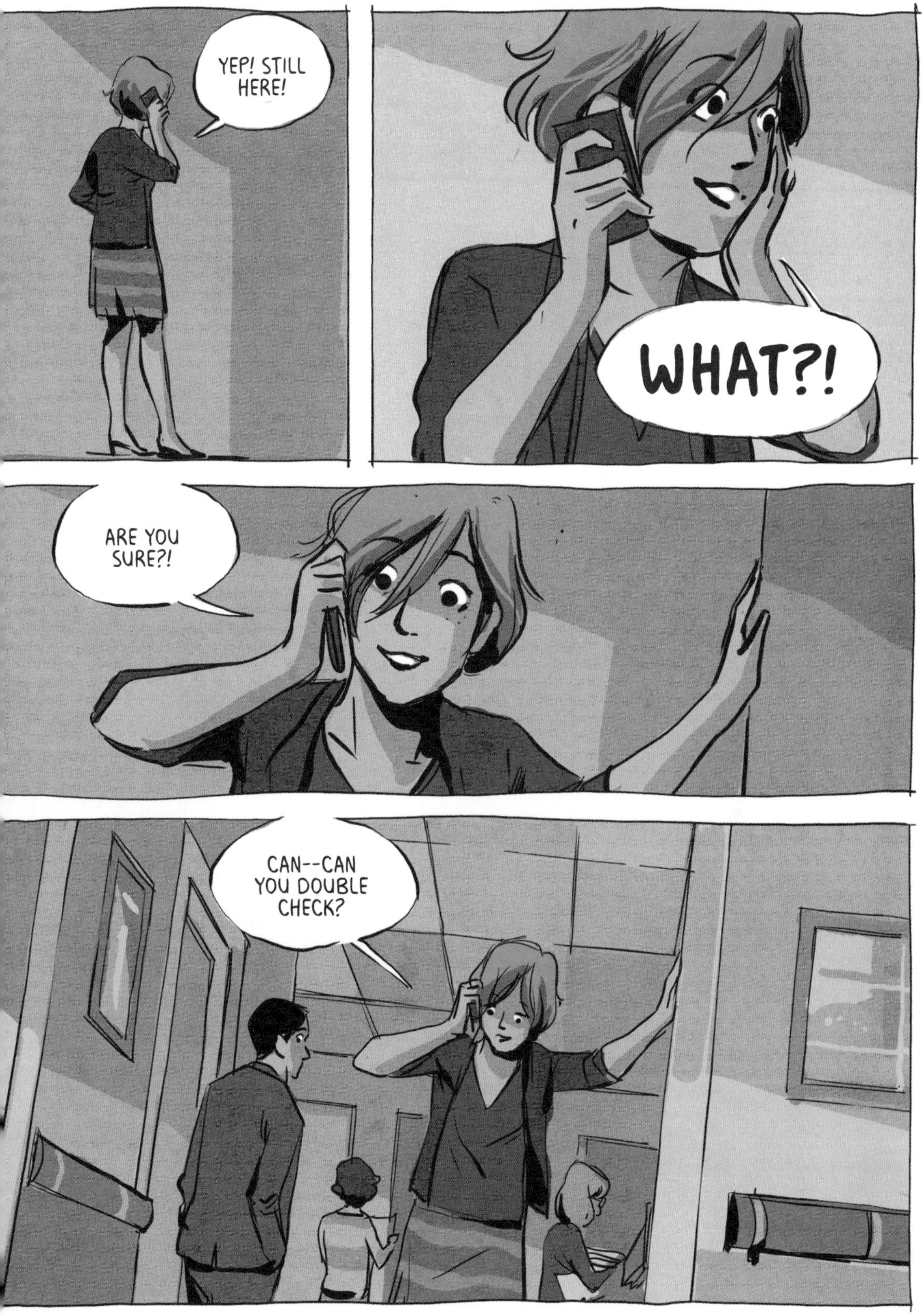
YEP! STILL HERE!
WHAT?!
ARE YOU SURE?!
CAN--CAN YOU DOUBLE CHECK?

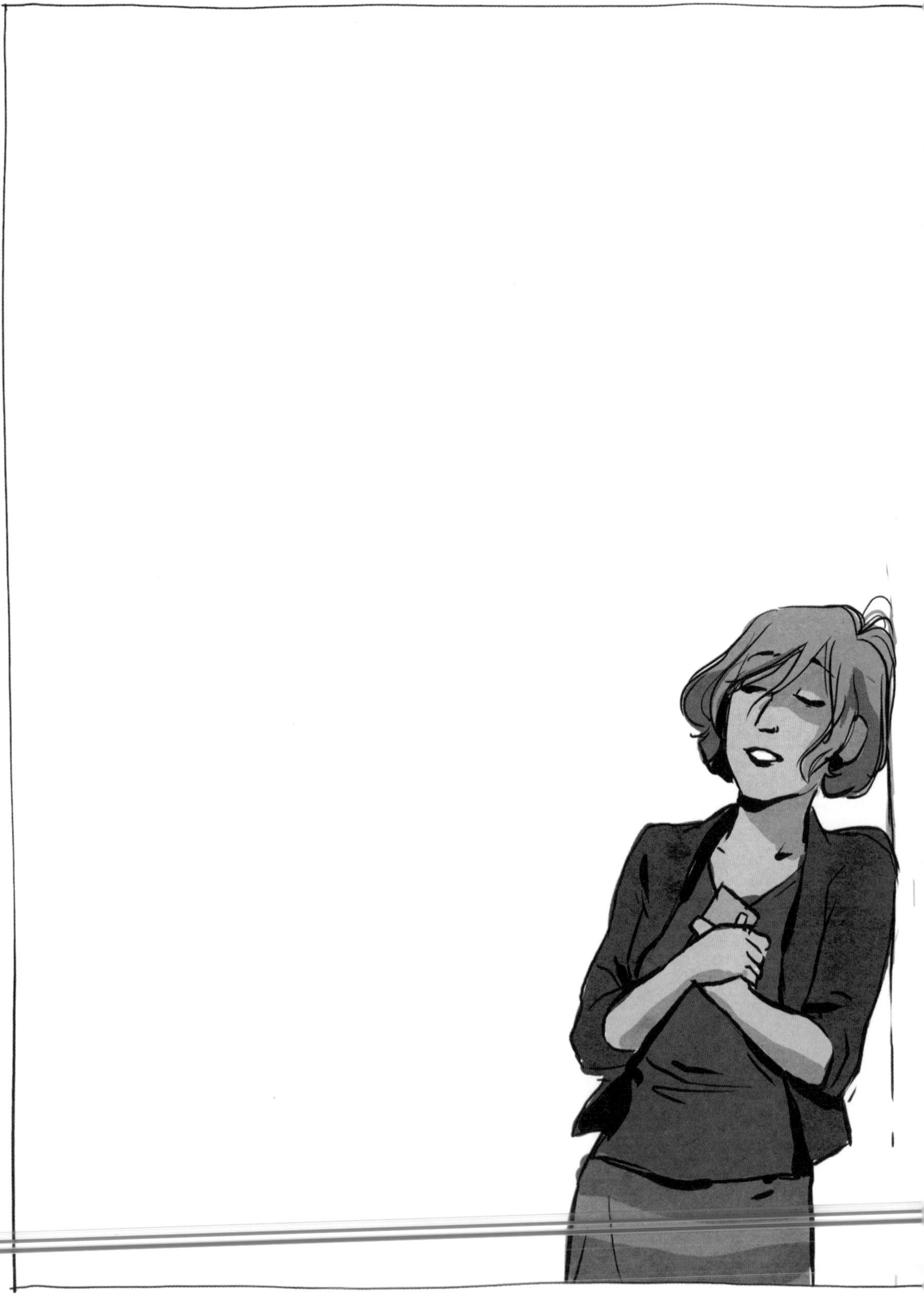

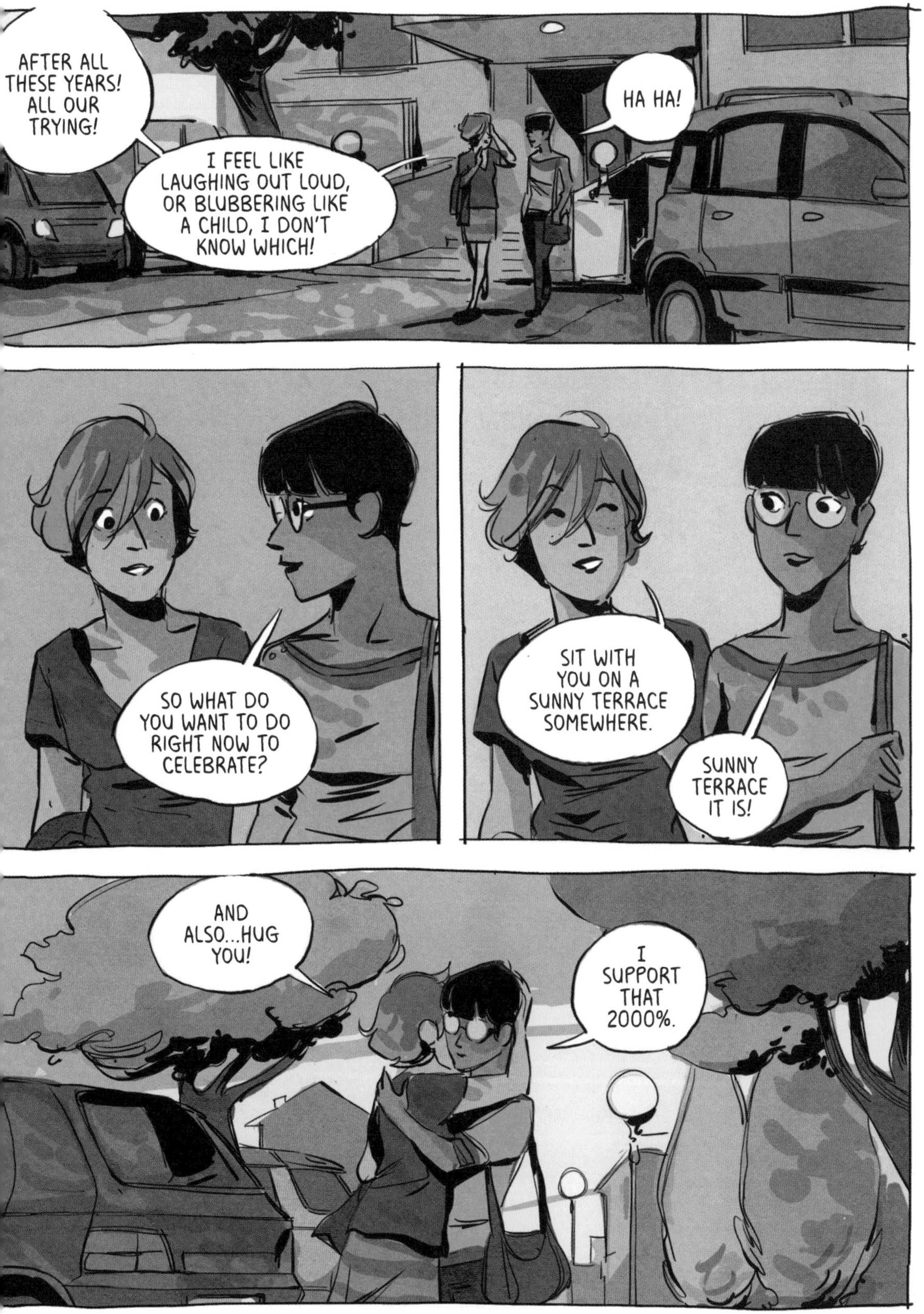
AFTER ALL THESE YEARS! ALL OUR TRYING!
I FEEL LIKE LAUGHING OUT LOUD, OR BLUBBERING LIKE A CHILD, I DON'T KNOW WHICH!
HA HA!
SO WHAT DO YOU WANT TO DO RIGHT NOW TO CELEBRATE?
SIT WITH YOU ON A SUNNY TERRACE SOMEWHERE.
SUNNY TERRACE IT IS!
AND ALSO...HUG YOU!
I SUPPORT THAT 2000%.

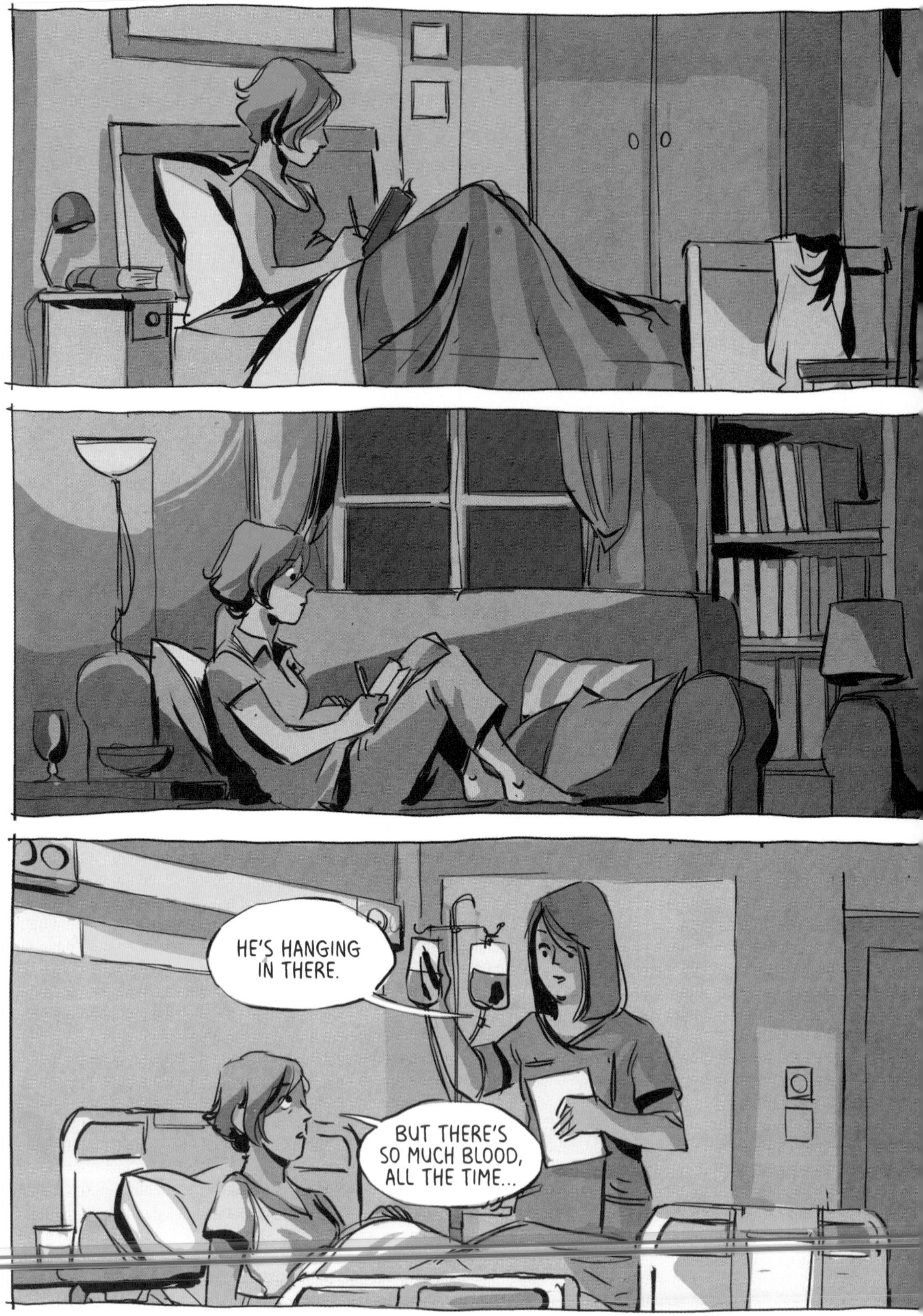
HE'S HANGING IN THERE.
BUT THERE'S SO MUCH BLOOD, ALL THE TIME...

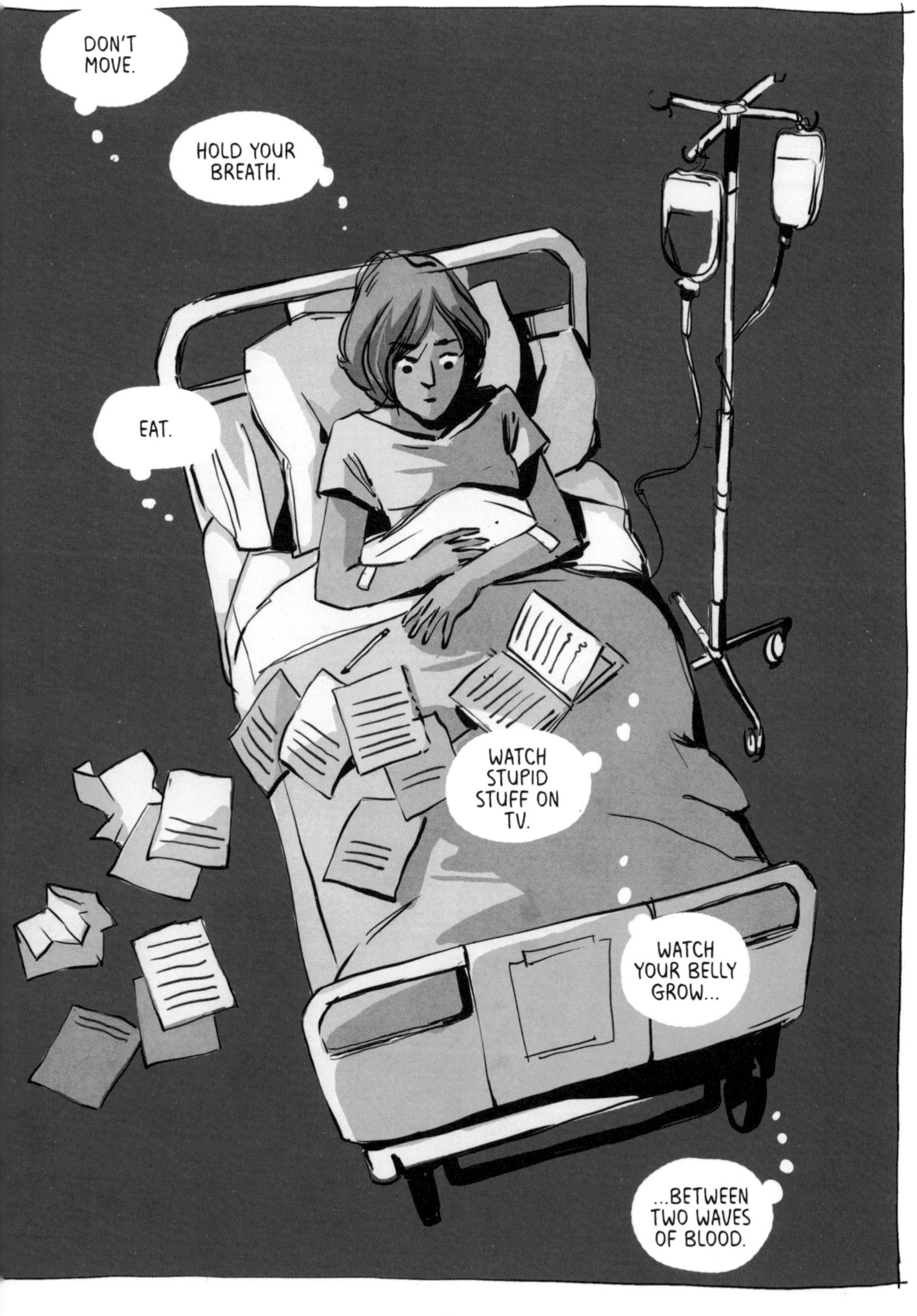
DON'T MOVE.
HOLD YOUR BREATH.
EAT.
WATCH STUPID STUFF ON TV.
WATCH YOUR BELLY GROW...
...BETWEEN TWO WAVES OF BLOOD.

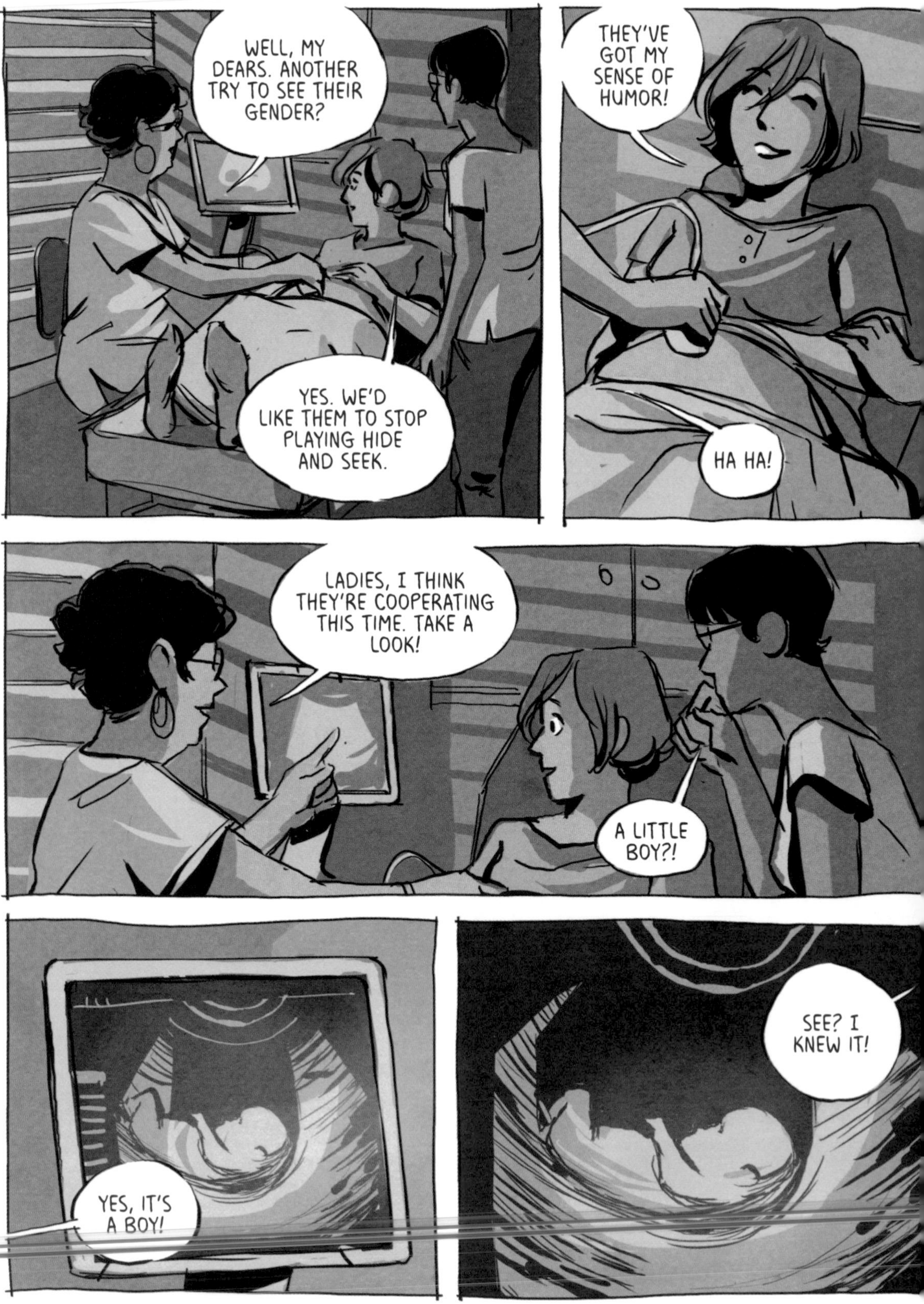
WELL, MY DEARS. ANOTHER TRY TO SEE THEIR GENDER?
YES. WE'D LIKE THEM TO STOP PLAYING HIDE AND SEEK.
THEY'VE GOT MY SENSE OF HUMOR!
HA HA!
LADIES, I THINK THEY'RE COOPERATING THIS TIME. TAKE A LOOK!
A LITTLE BOY?!
YES, IT'S A BOY!
SEE? I KNEW IT!

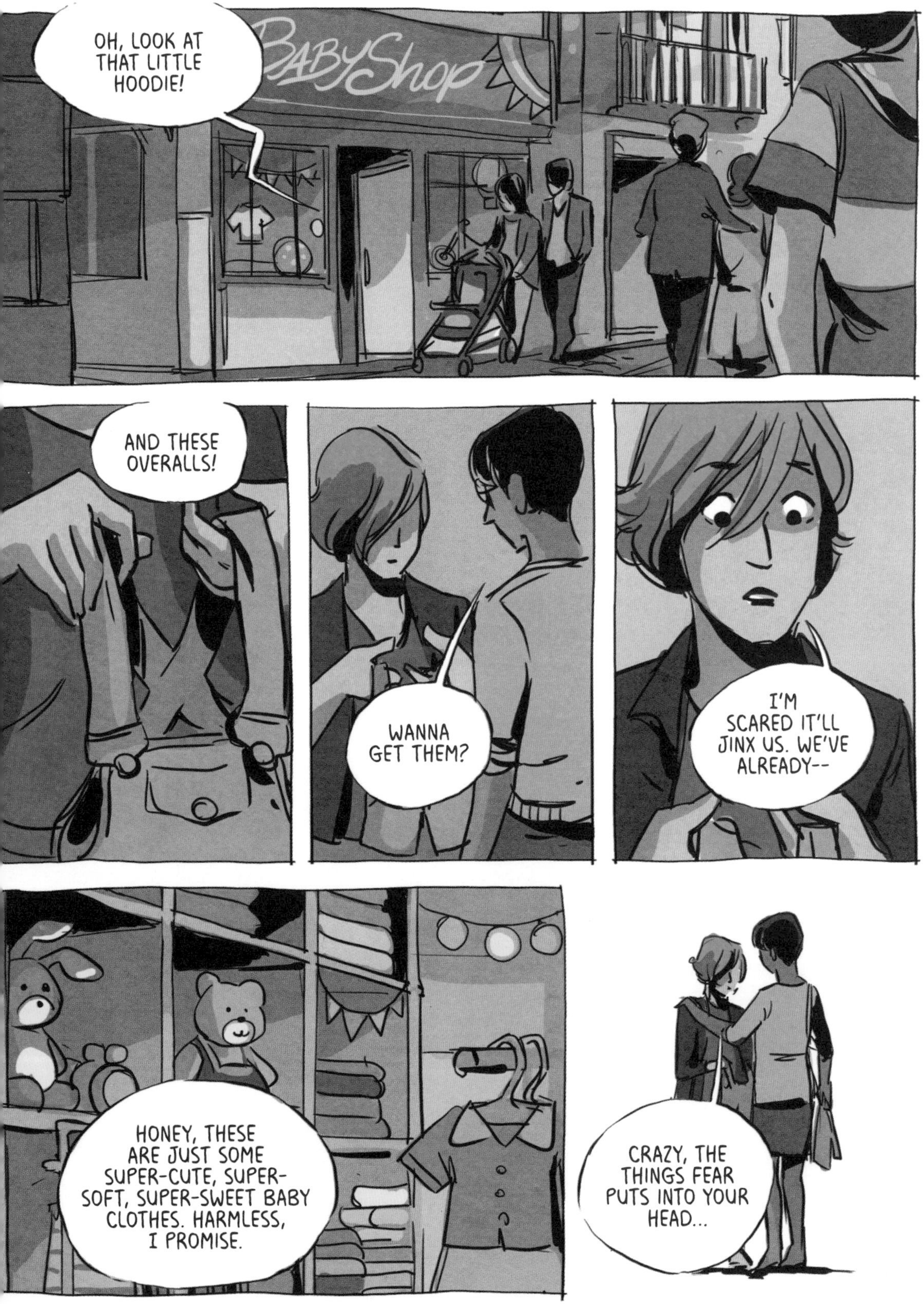
BABY Shop
OH, LOOK AT THAT LITTLE HOODIE!
AND THESE OVERALLS!
WANNA GET THEM?
I'M SCARED IT'LL JINX US. WE'VE ALREADY--
HONEY, THESE ARE JUST SOME SUPER-CUTE, SUPER-SOFT, SUPER-SWEET BABY CLOTHES. HARMLESS, I PROMISE.
CRAZY, THE THINGS FEAR PUTS INTO YOUR HEAD...

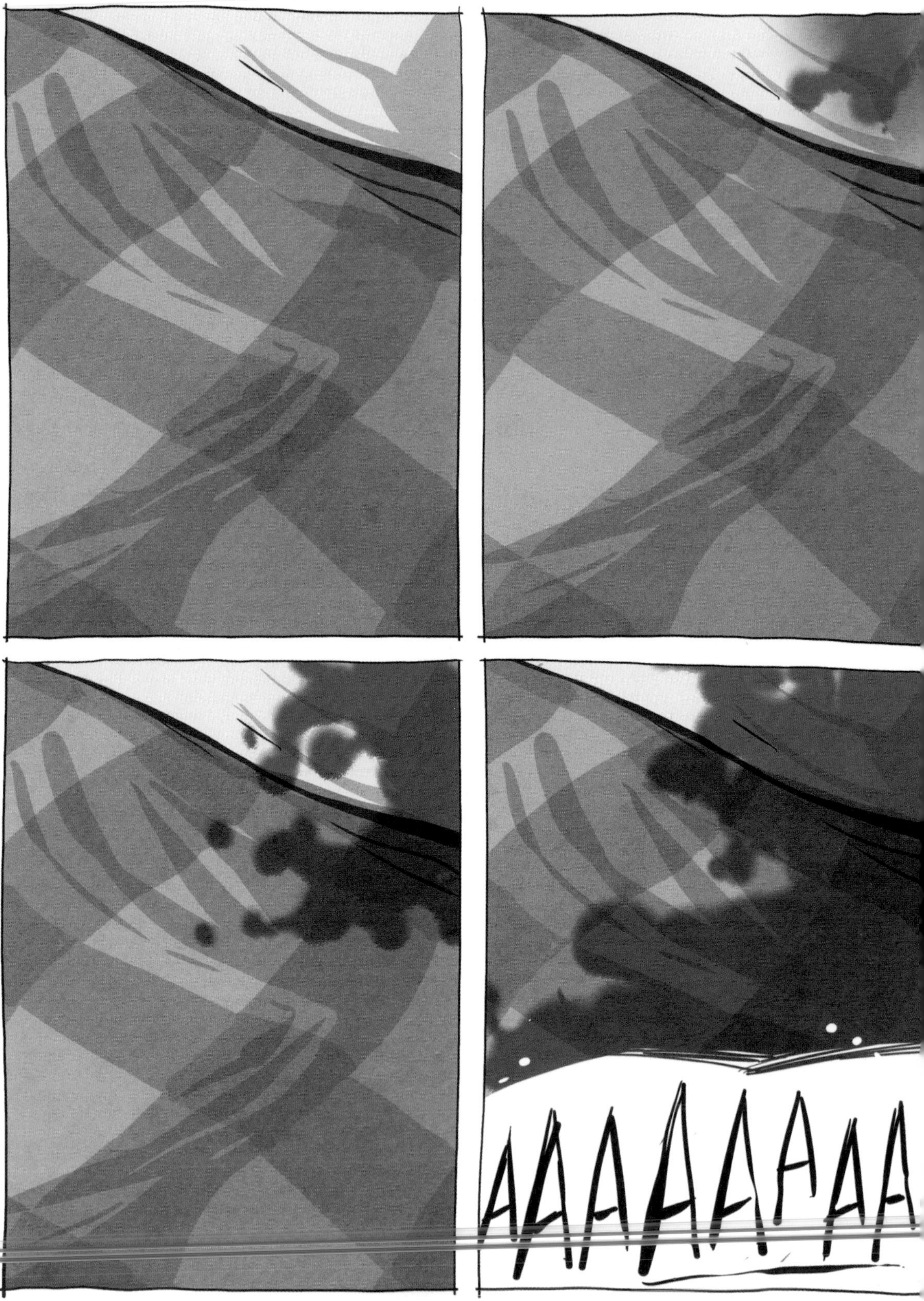
AAAAAAAAA

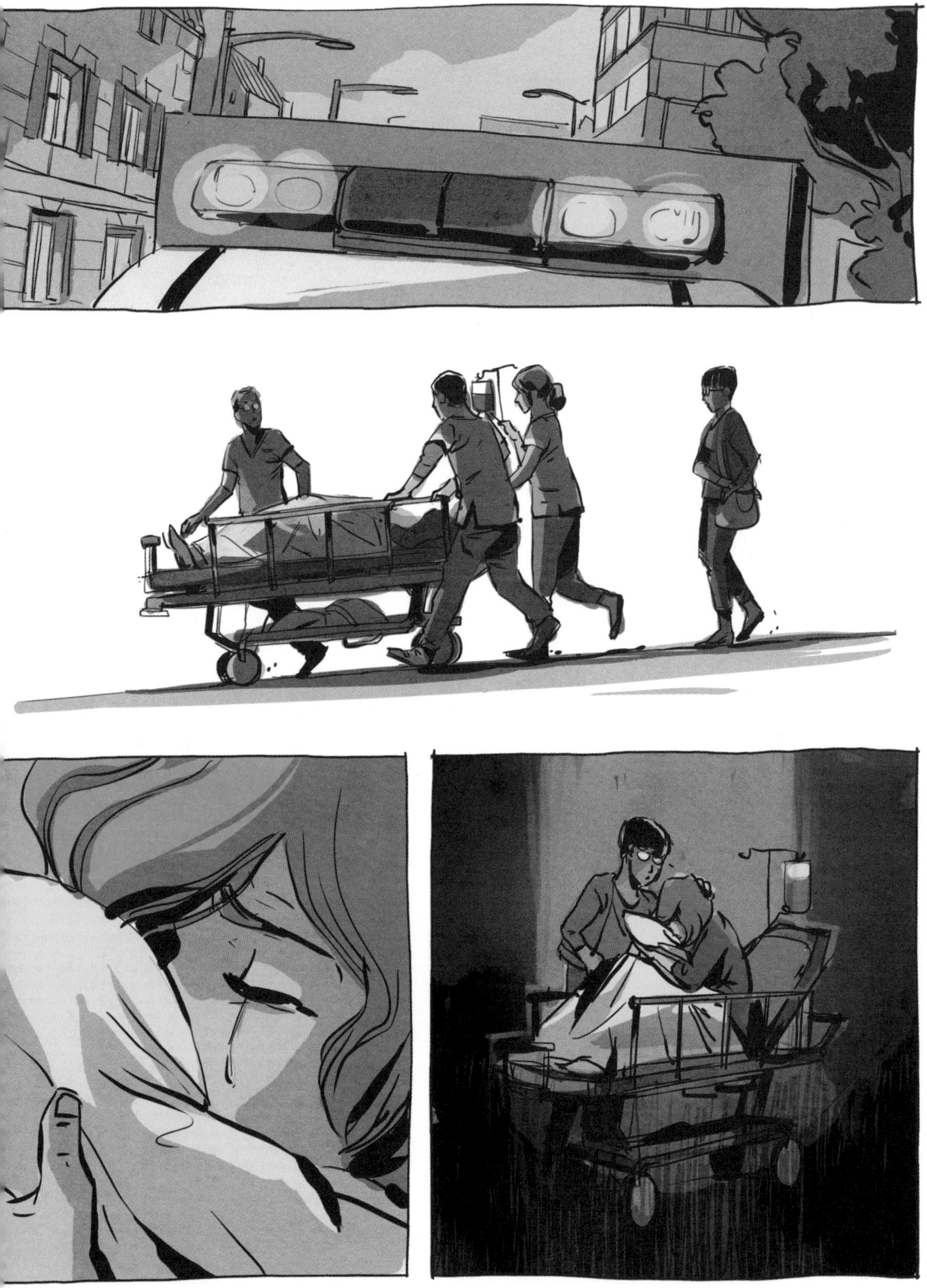

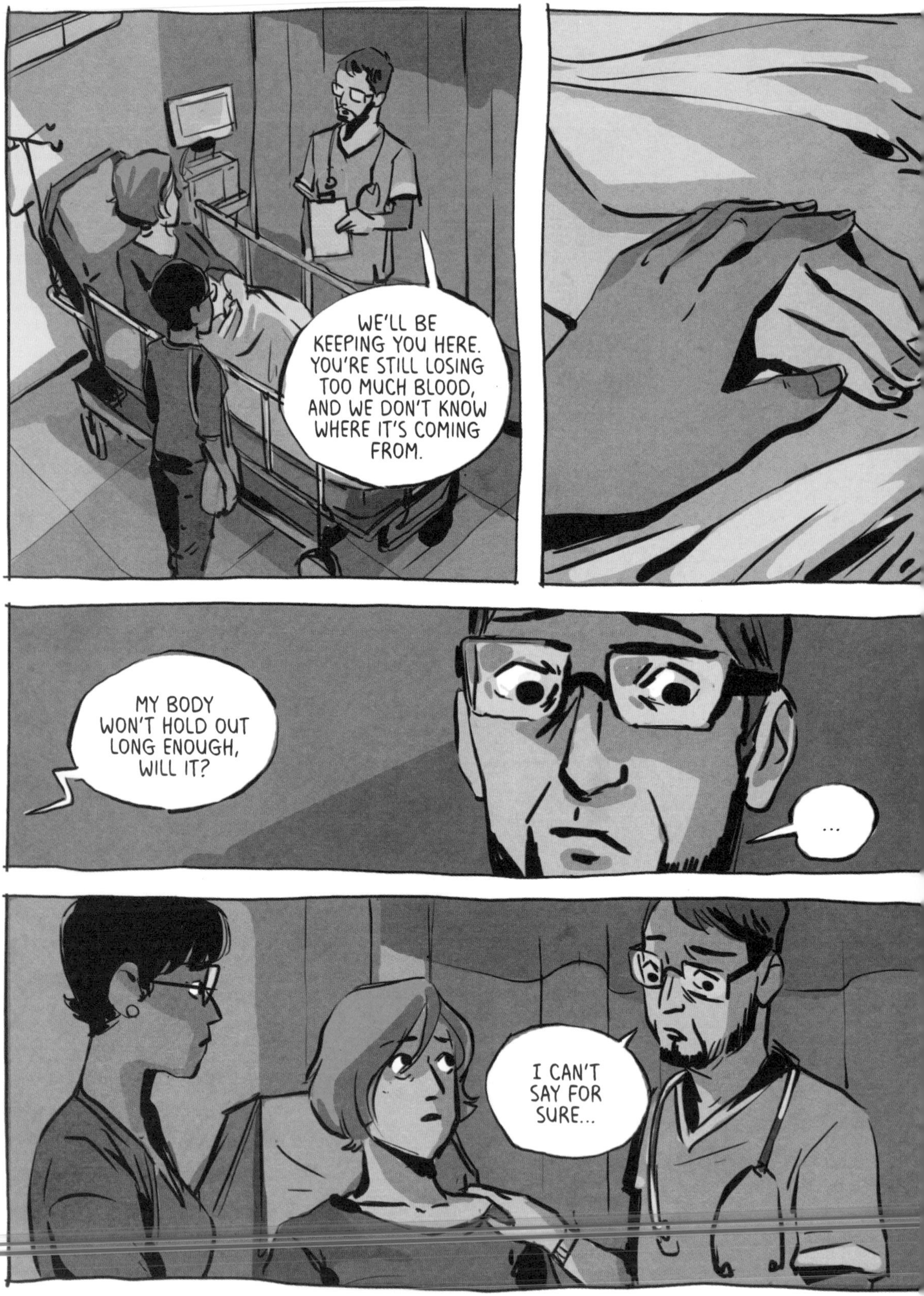
WE'LL BE KEEPING YOU HERE. YOU'RE STILL LOSING TOO MUCH BLOOD, AND WE DON'T KNOW WHERE IT'S COMING FROM.
MY BODY WON'T HOLD OUT LONG ENOUGH, WILL IT?
...
I CAN'T SAY FOR SURE...

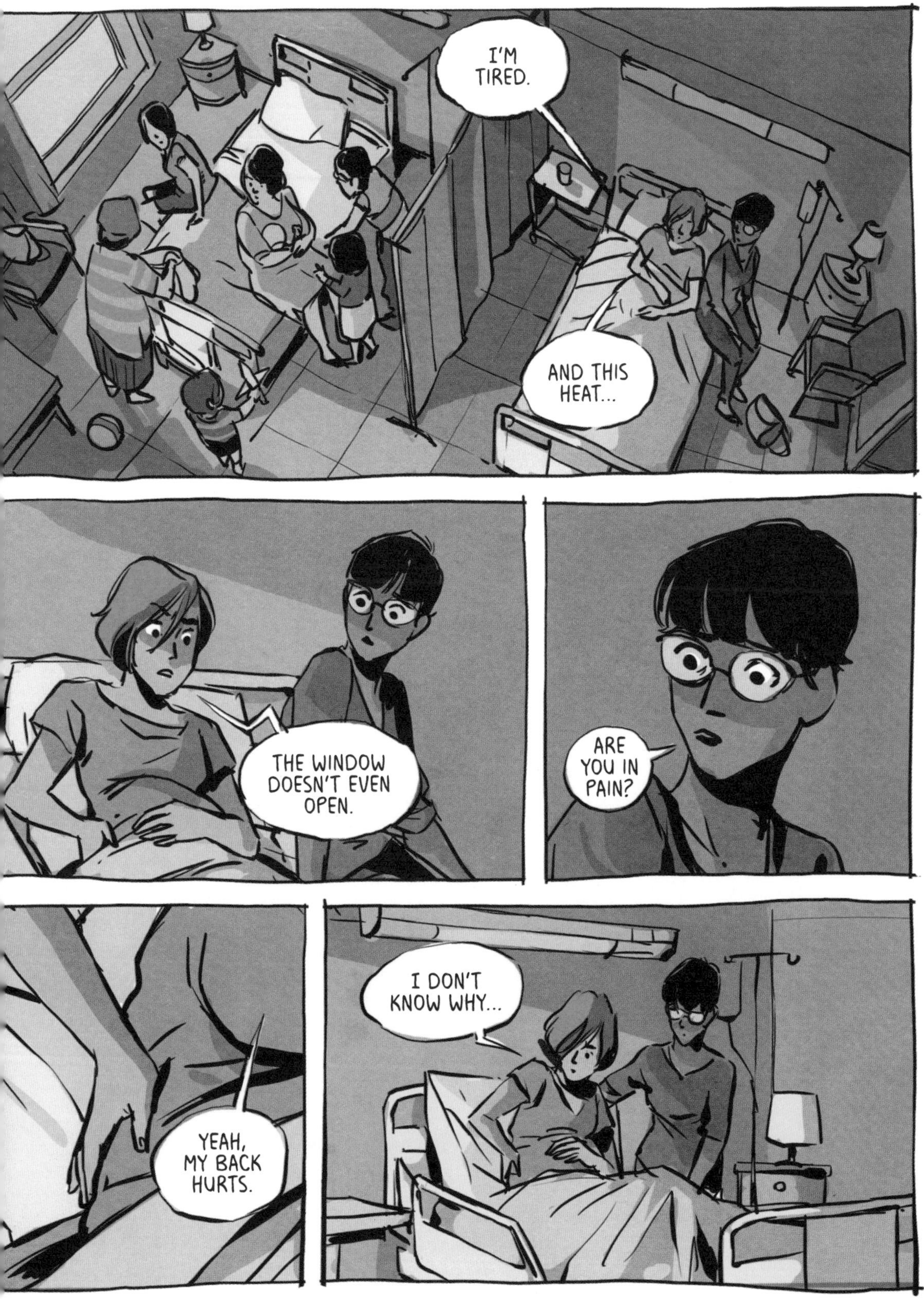
I'M TIRED.
AND THIS HEAT...
THE WINDOW DOESN'T EVEN OPEN.
ARE YOU IN PAIN?
YEAH, MY BACK HURTS.
I DON'T KNOW WHY...

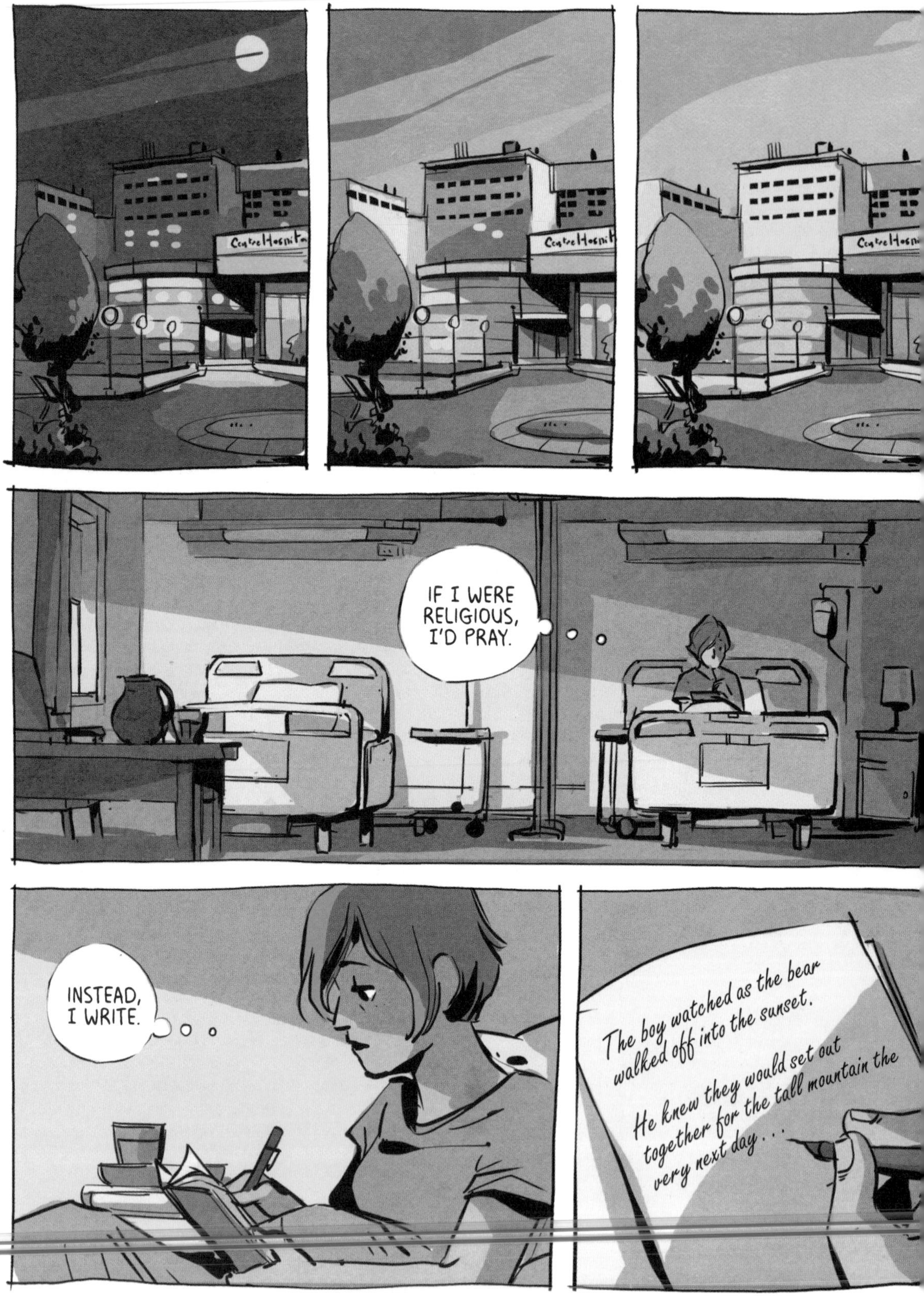
IF I WERE RELIGIOUS, I'D PRAY.
INSTEAD, I WRITE.
The boy watched as the bear walked off into the sunset.
He knew they would set out together for the tall mountain the very next day . . .

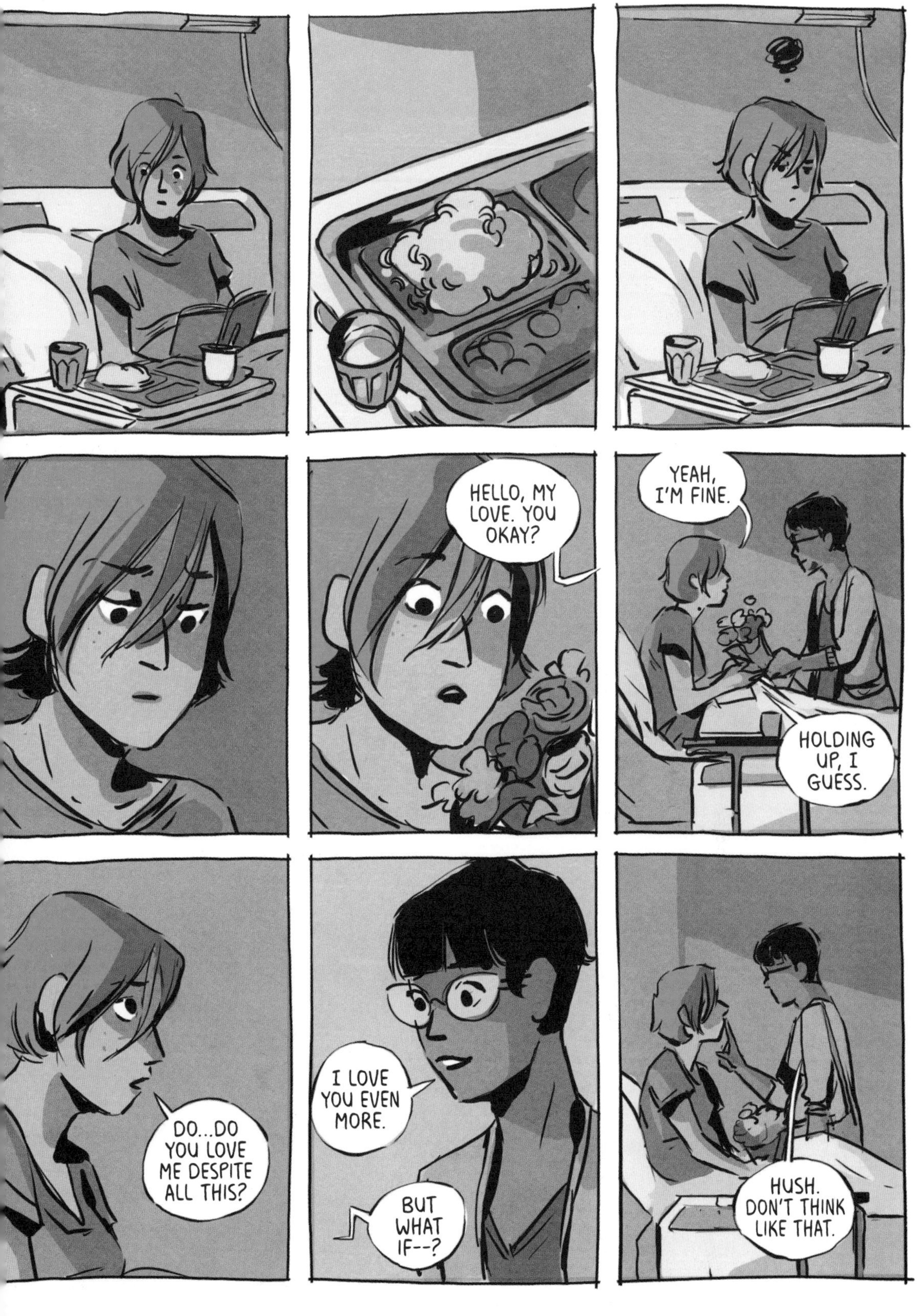
HELLO, MY LOVE. YOU OKAY?
YEAH, I'M FINE.
HOLDING UP, I GUESS.
DO...DO YOU LOVE ME DESPITE ALL THIS?
I LOVE YOU EVEN MORE.
BUT WHAT IF--?
HUSH. DON'T THINK LIKE THAT.

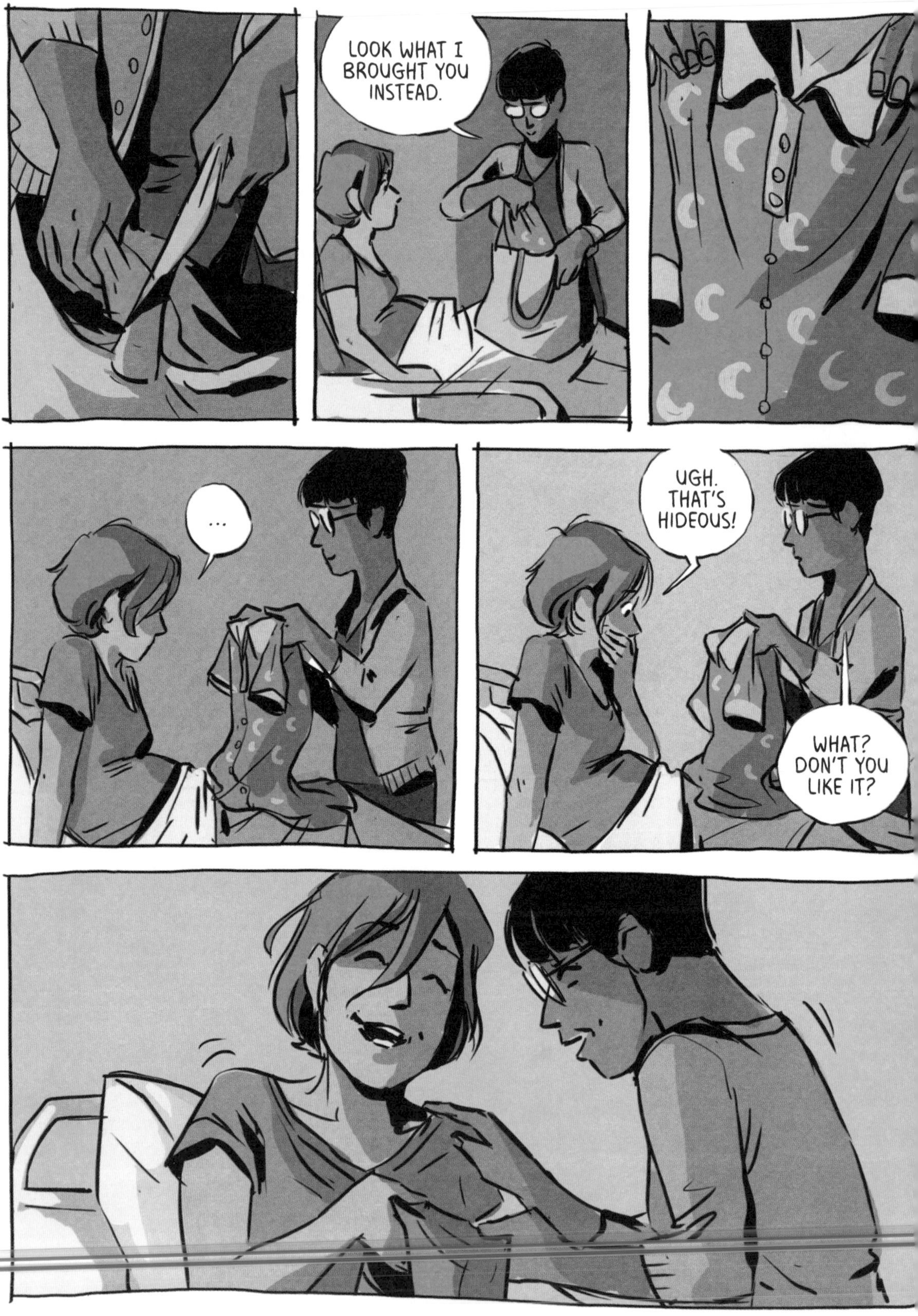
LOOK WHAT I BROUGHT YOU INSTEAD.
...
UGH. THAT'S HIDEOUS!
WHAT? DON'T YOU LIKE IT?

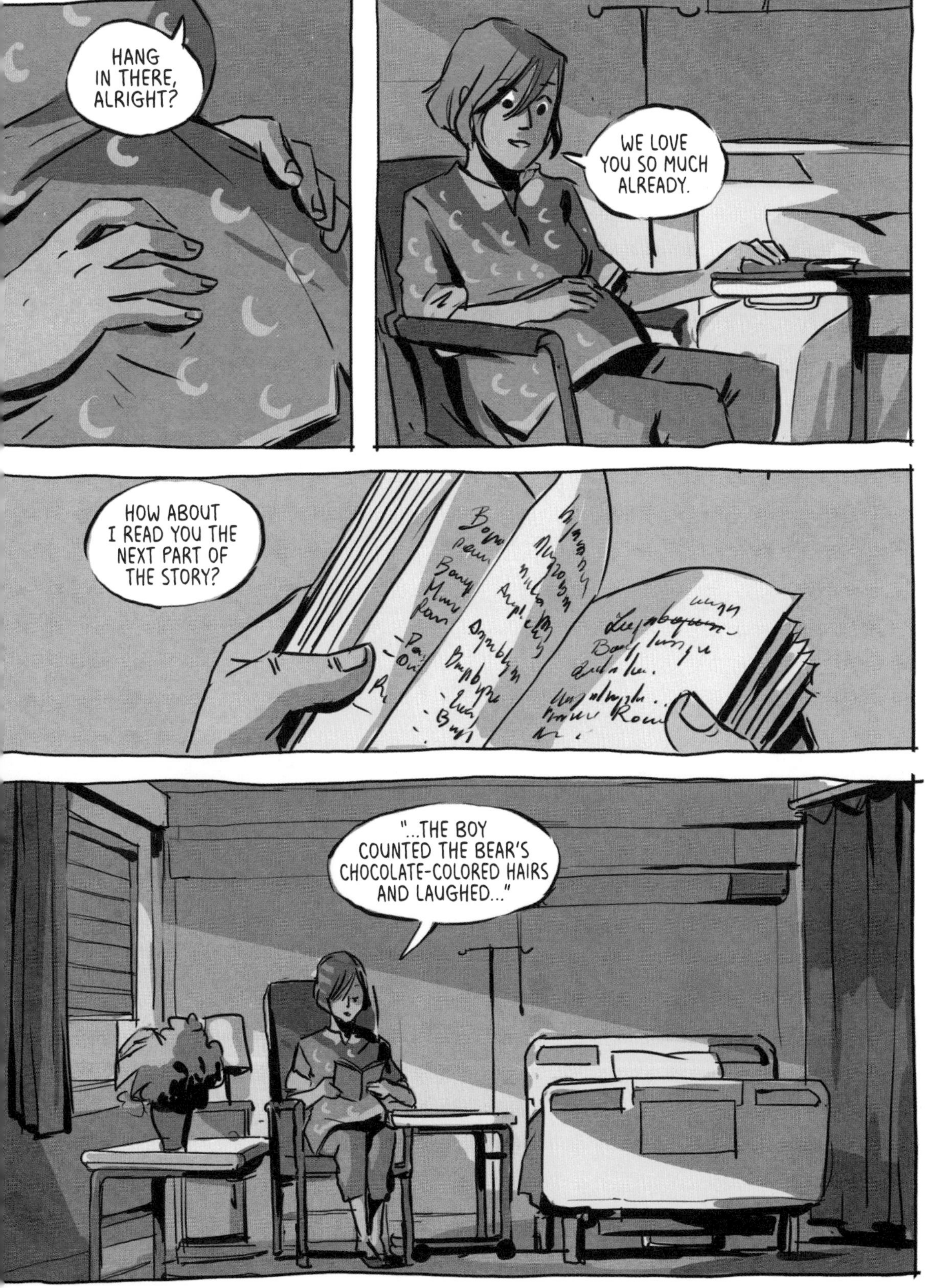
HANG IN THERE, ALRIGHT?
WE LOVE YOU SO MUCH ALREADY.
HOW ABOUT I READ YOU THE NEXT PART OF THE STORY?
"...THE BOY COUNTED THE BEAR'S CHOCOLATE-COLORED HAIRS AND LAUGHED..."

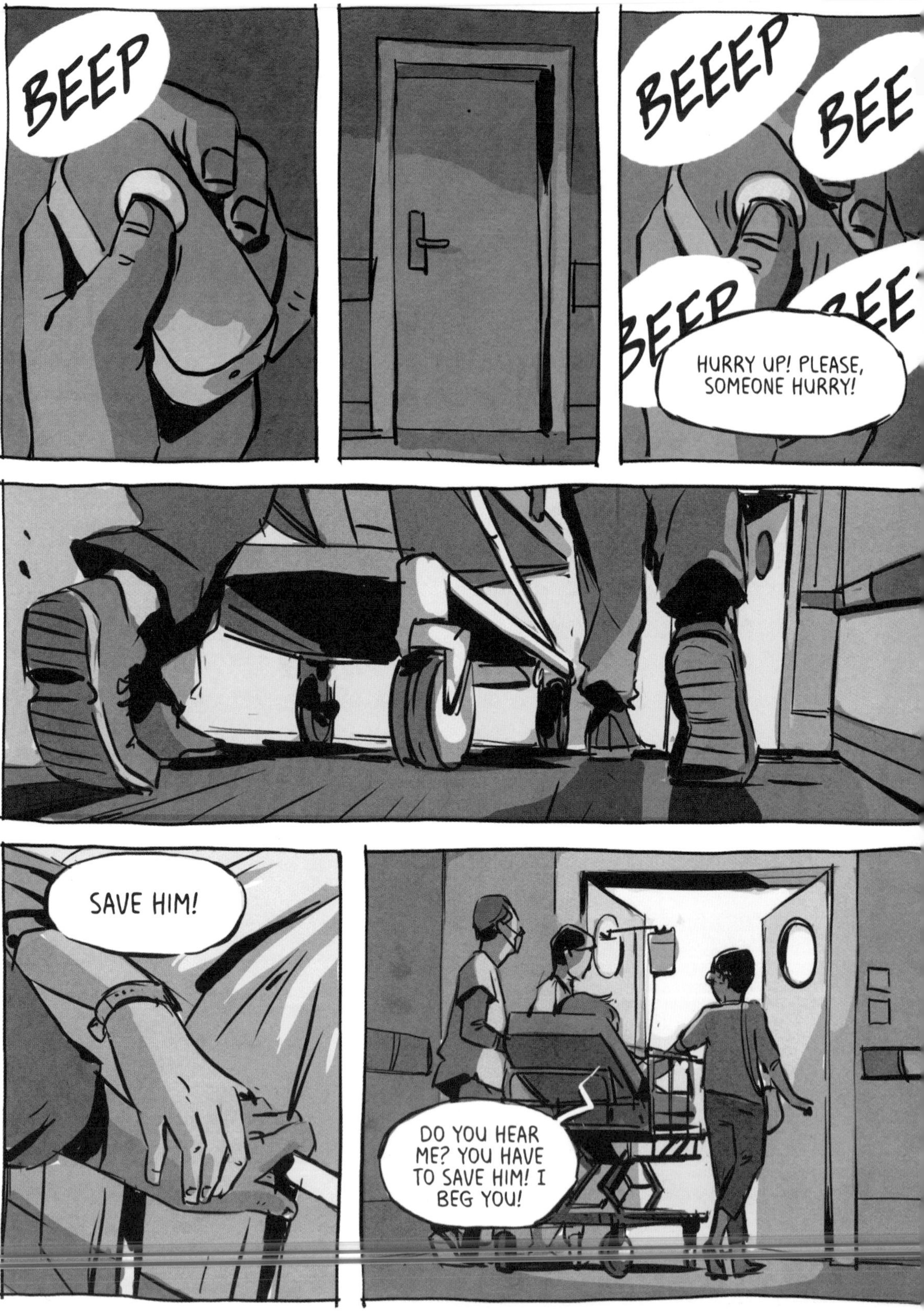
BEEP
BEEEP
BEE
BEEP
BEE
HURRY UP! PLEASE, SOMEONE HURRY!
SAVE HIM!
DO YOU HEAR ME? YOU HAVE TO SAVE HIM! I BEG YOU!

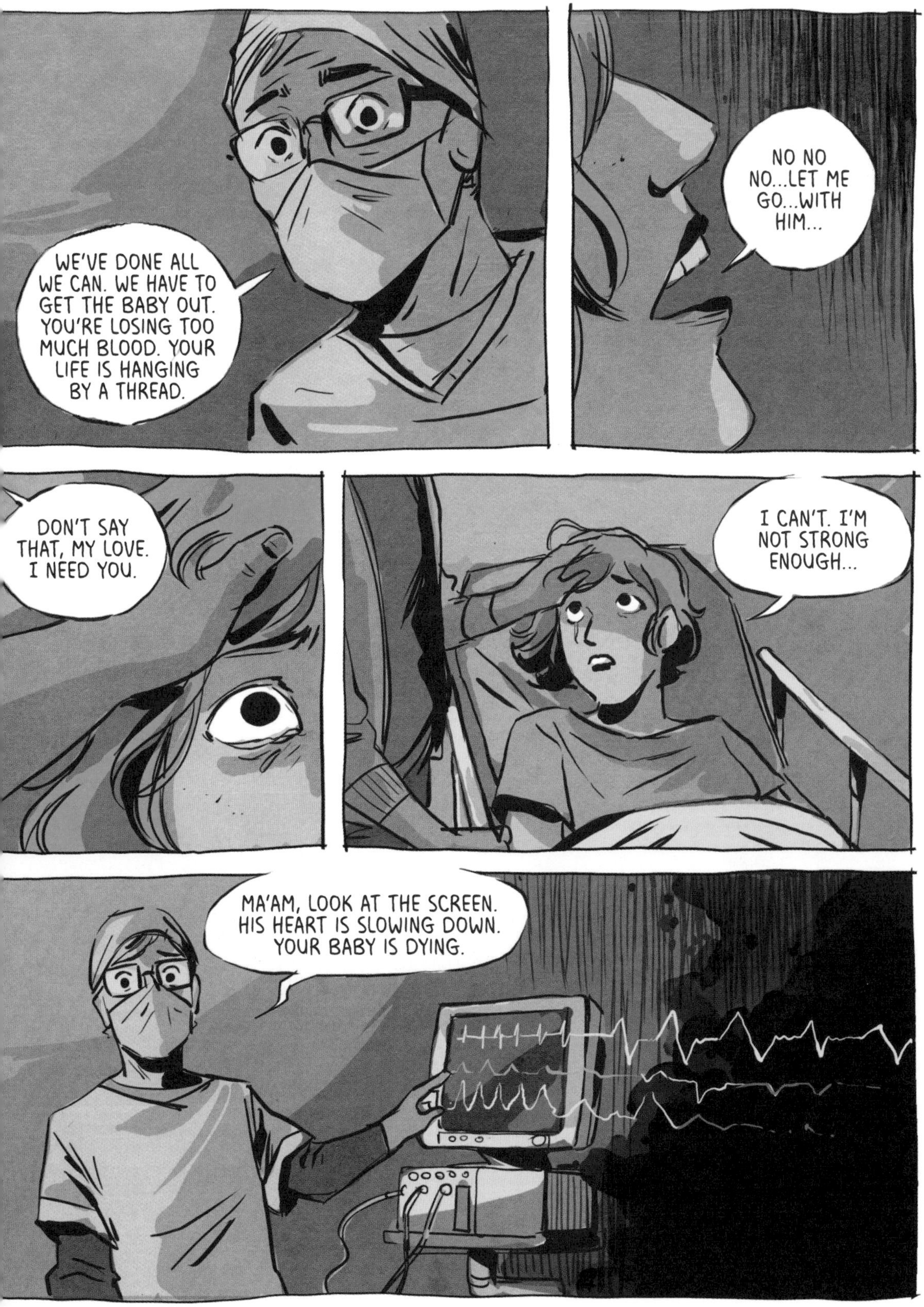
WE'VE DONE ALL WE CAN. WE HAVE TO GET THE BABY OUT. YOU'RE LOSING TOO MUCH BLOOD. YOUR LIFE IS HANGING BY A THREAD.
NO NO NO...LET ME GO...WITH HIM...
DON'T SAY THAT, MY LOVE. I NEED YOU.
I CAN'T. I'M NOT STRONG ENOUGH...
MA'AM, LOOK AT THE SCREEN. HIS HEART IS SLOWING DOWN. YOUR BABY IS DYING.

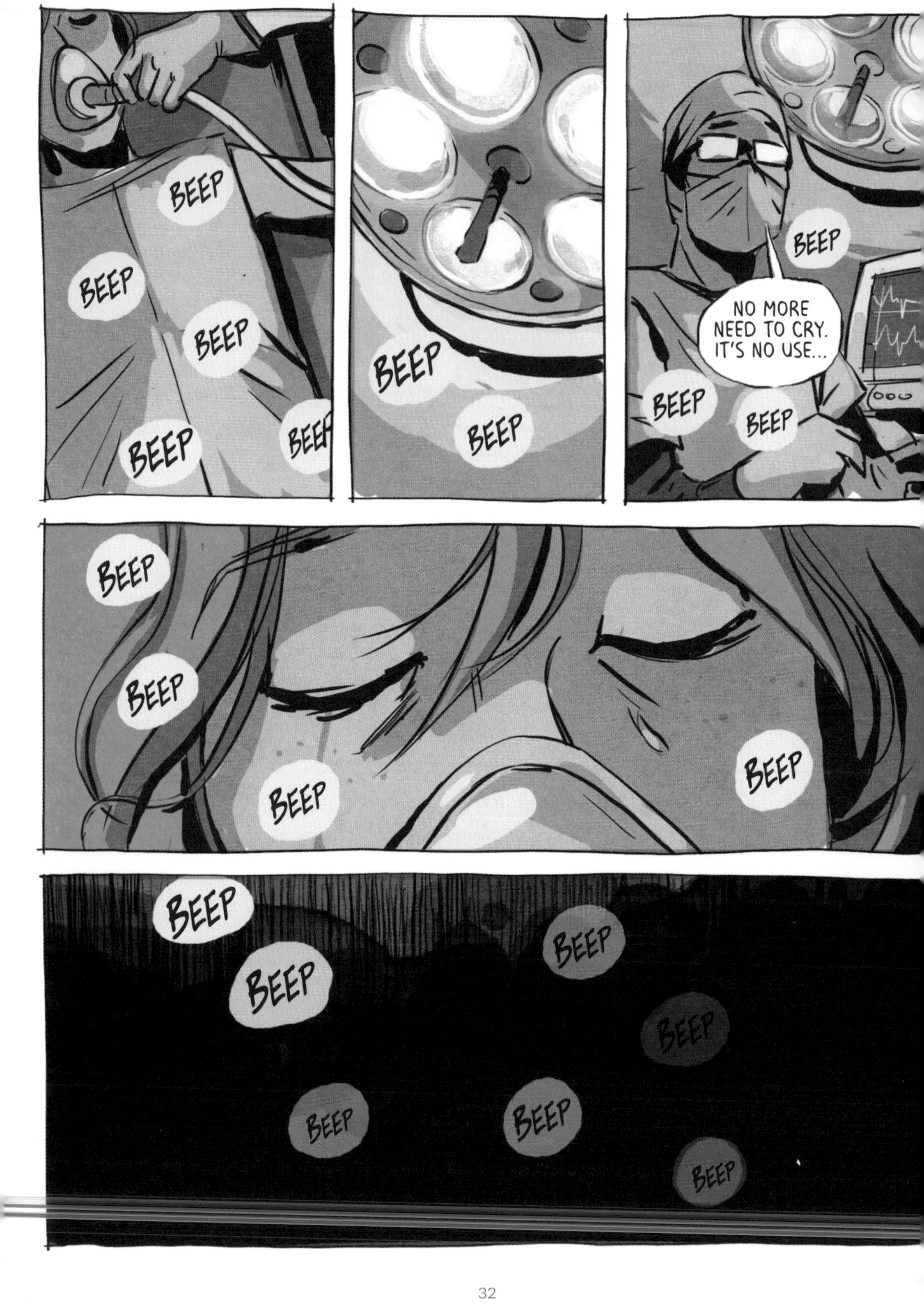
BEEP
BEEP
BEEP
BEEP
BEEP
BEEP
BEEP
NO MORE NEED TO CRY. IT'S NO USE...
BEEP
BEEP
BEEP
BEEP
BEEP
BEEP
BEEP
BEEP
BEEP
BEEP
BEEP
BEEP
BEEP
BEEP

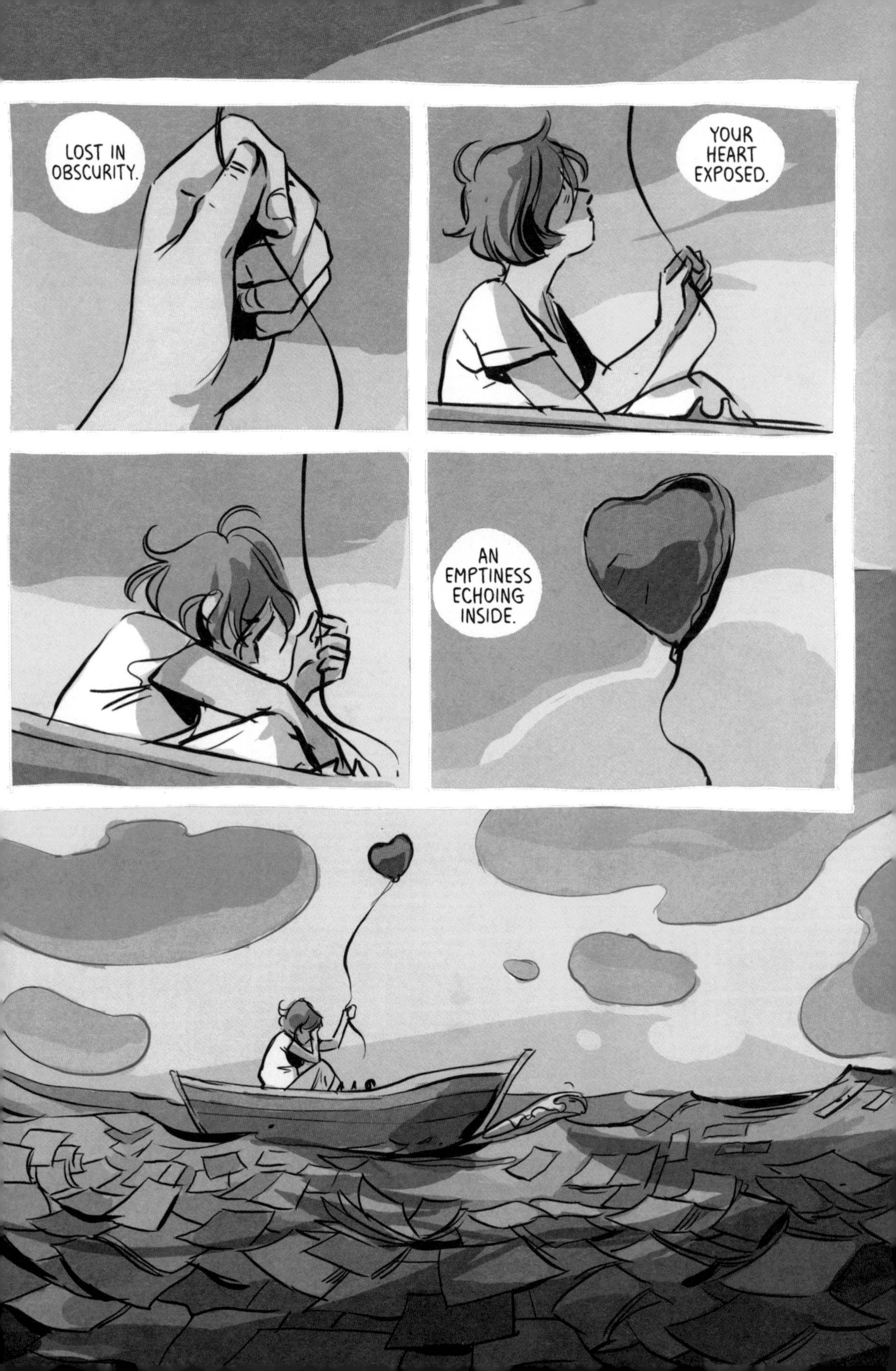
LOST IN OBSCURITY.
YOUR HEART EXPOSED.
AN EMPTINESS ECHOING INSIDE.

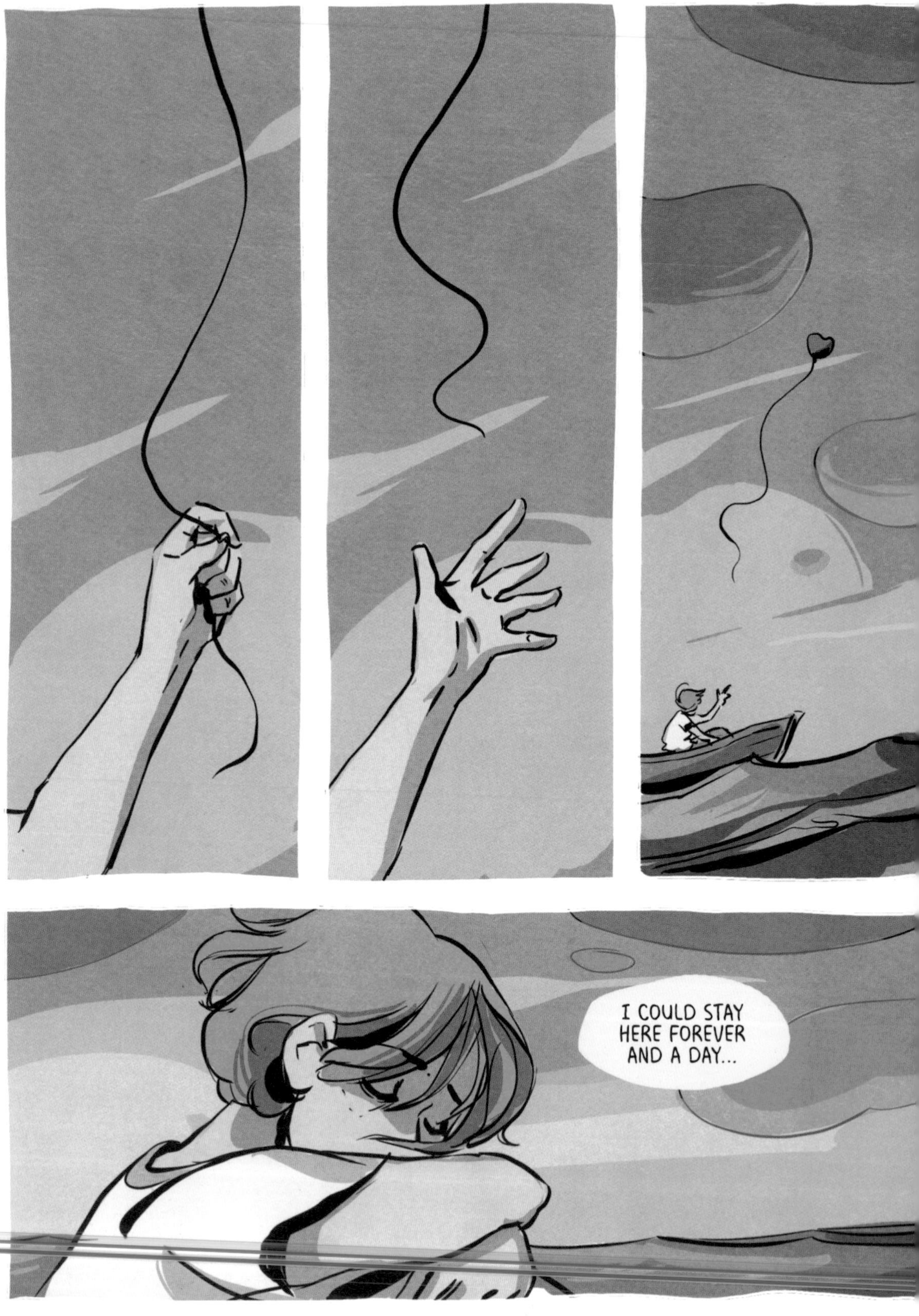
I COULD STAY HERE FOREVER AND A DAY...

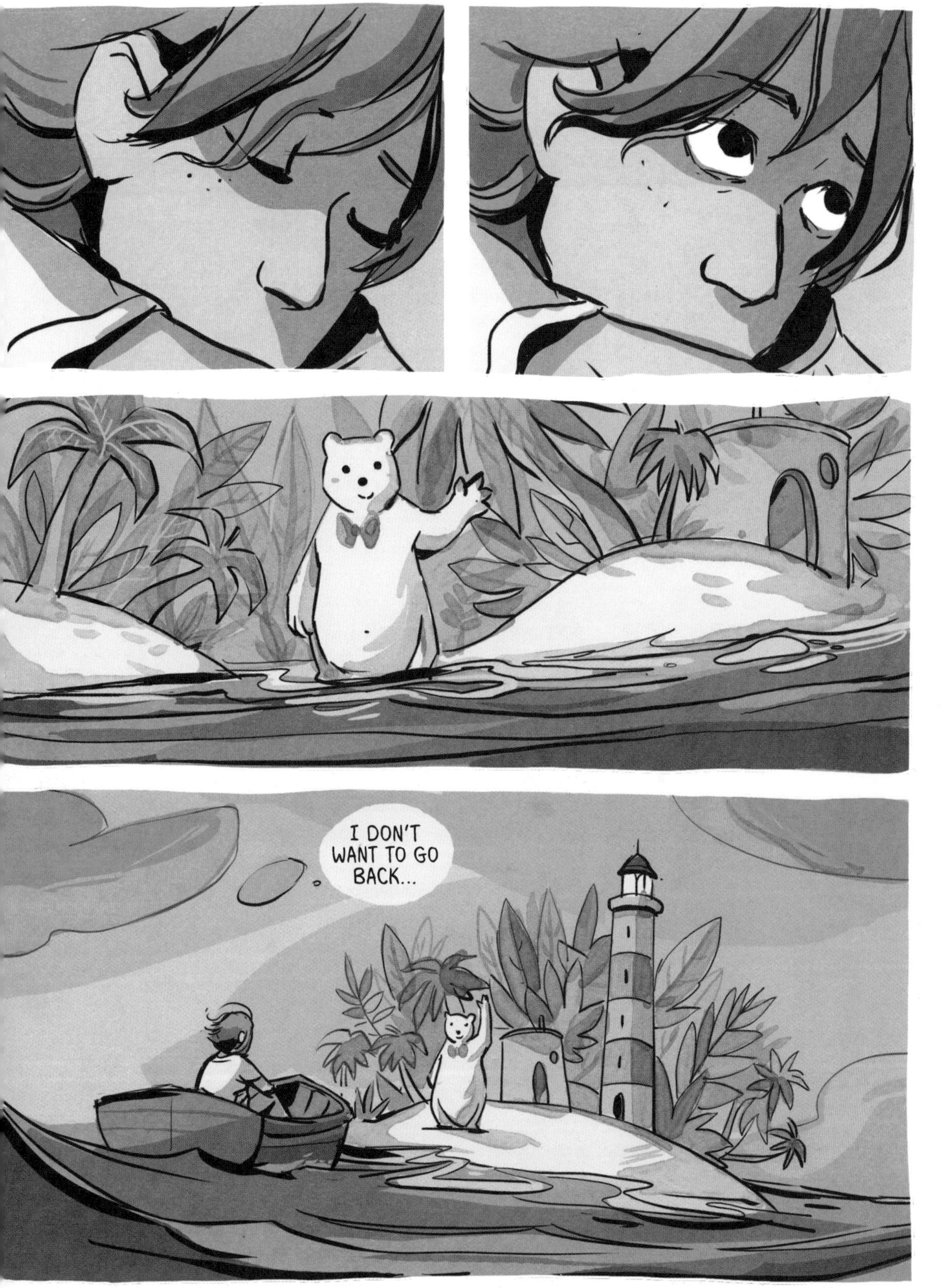
I DON'T WANT TO GO BACK...

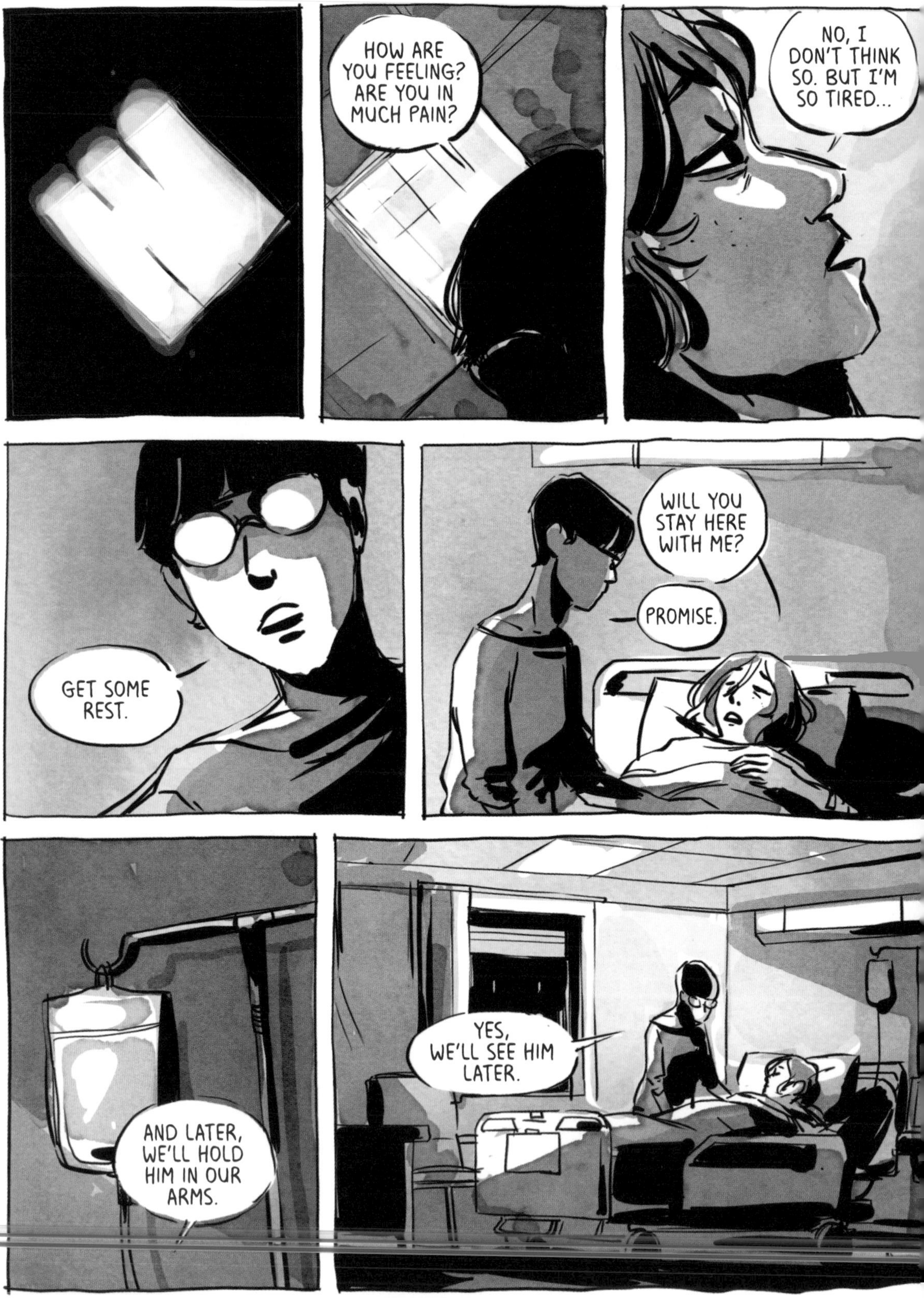
HOW ARE YOU FEELING? ARE YOU IN MUCH PAIN?
NO, I DON'T THINK SO. BUT I'M SO TIRED...
GET SOME REST.
WILL YOU STAY HERE WITH ME?
PROMISE.
AND LATER, WE'LL HOLD HIM IN OUR ARMS.
YES, WE'LL SEE HIM LATER.

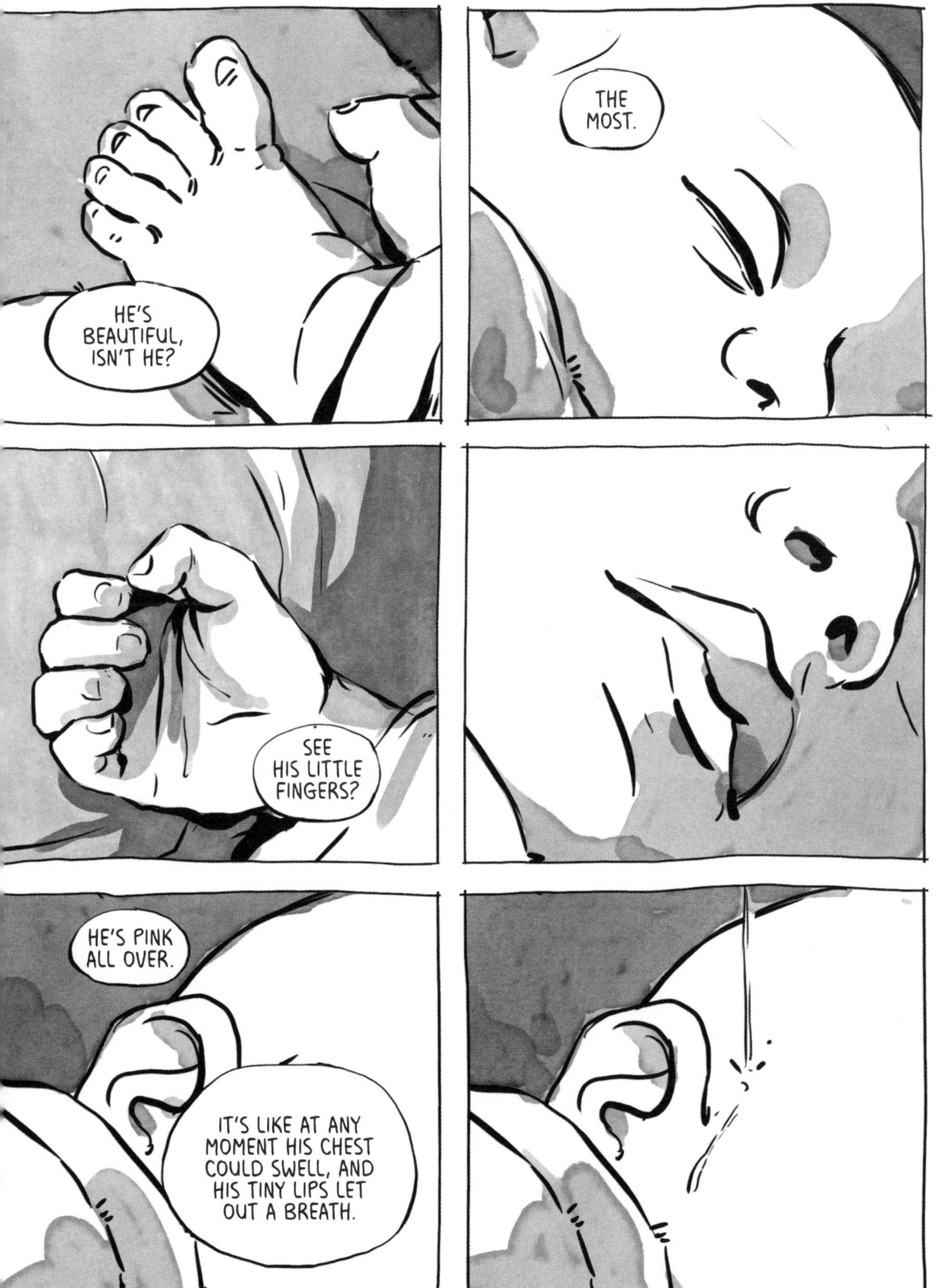
HE'S BEAUTIFUL, ISN'T HE?
THE MOST.
SEE HIS LITTLE FINGERS?
HE'S PINK ALL OVER.
IT'S LIKE AT ANY MOMENT HIS CHEST COULD SWELL, AND HIS TINY LIPS LET OUT A BREATH.

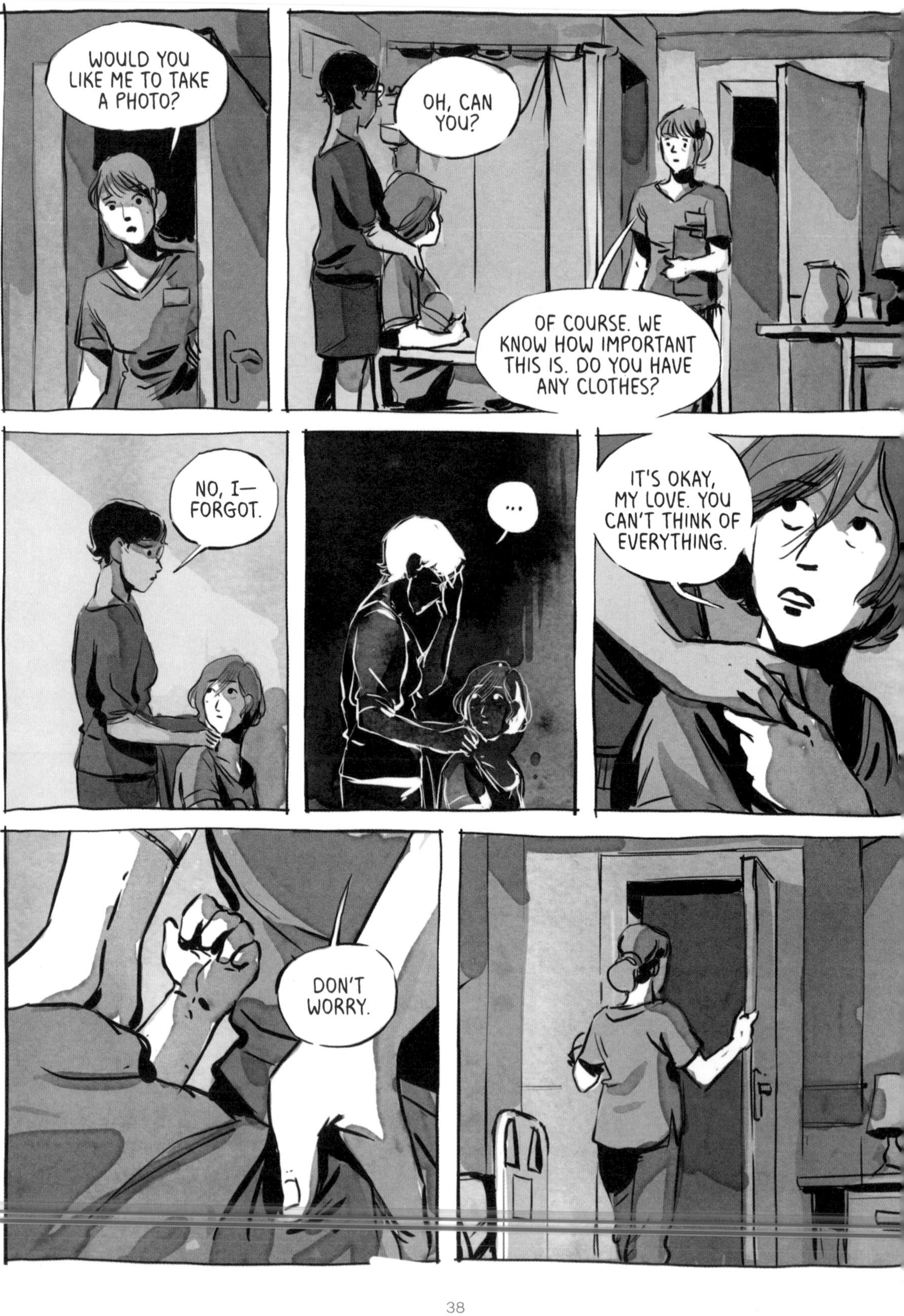
WOULD YOU LIKE ME TO TAKE A PHOTO?
OH, CAN YOU?
OF COURSE. WE KNOW HOW IMPORTANT THIS IS. DO YOU HAVE ANY CLOTHES?
NO, I— FORGOT.
...
IT'S OKAY, MY LOVE. YOU CAN'T THINK OF EVERYTHING.
DON'T WORRY.

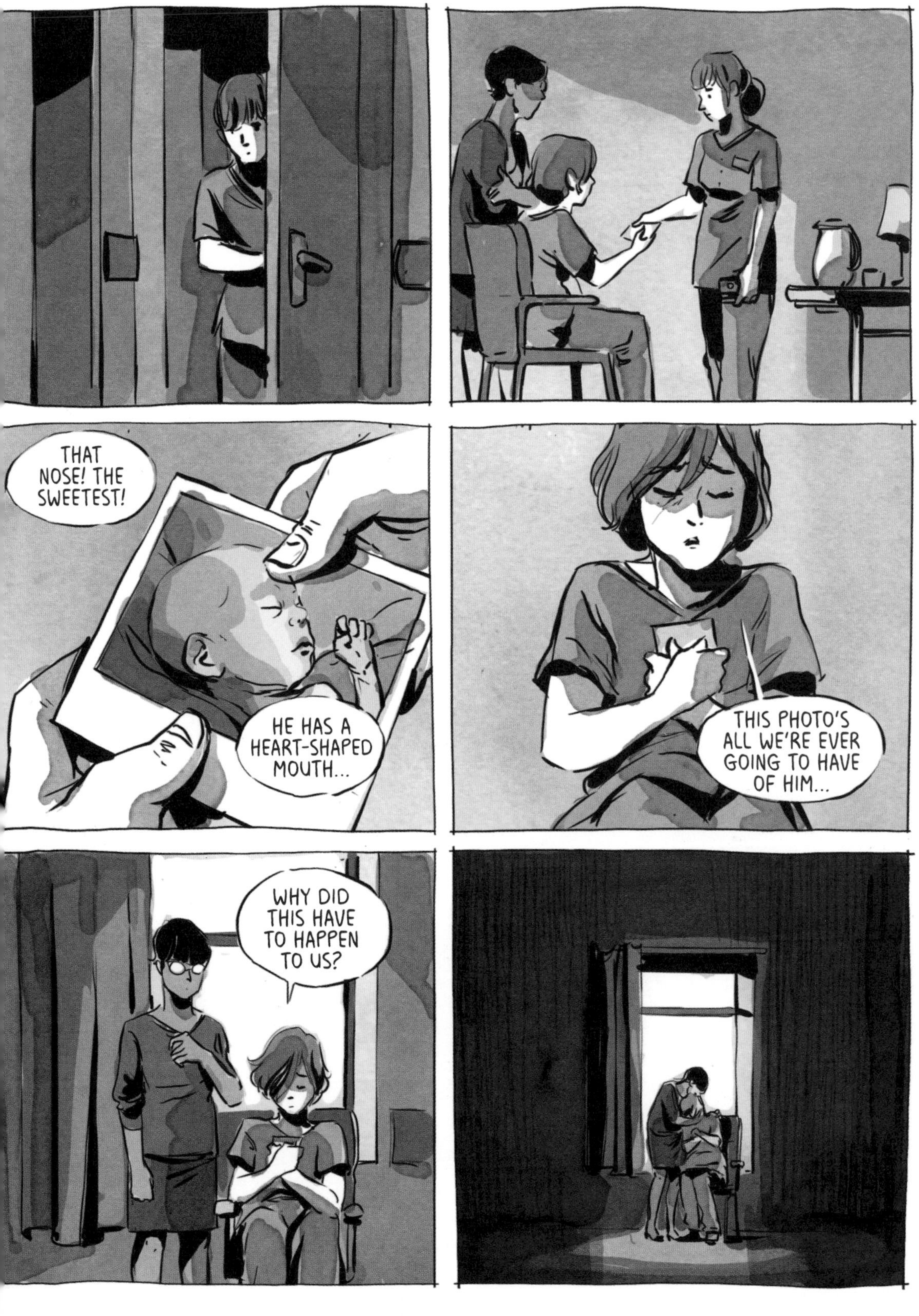
THAT NOSE! THE SWEETEST!
HE HAS A HEART-SHAPED MOUTH...
THIS PHOTO'S ALL WE'RE EVER GOING TO HAVE OF HIM...
WHY DID THIS HAVE TO HAPPEN TO US?

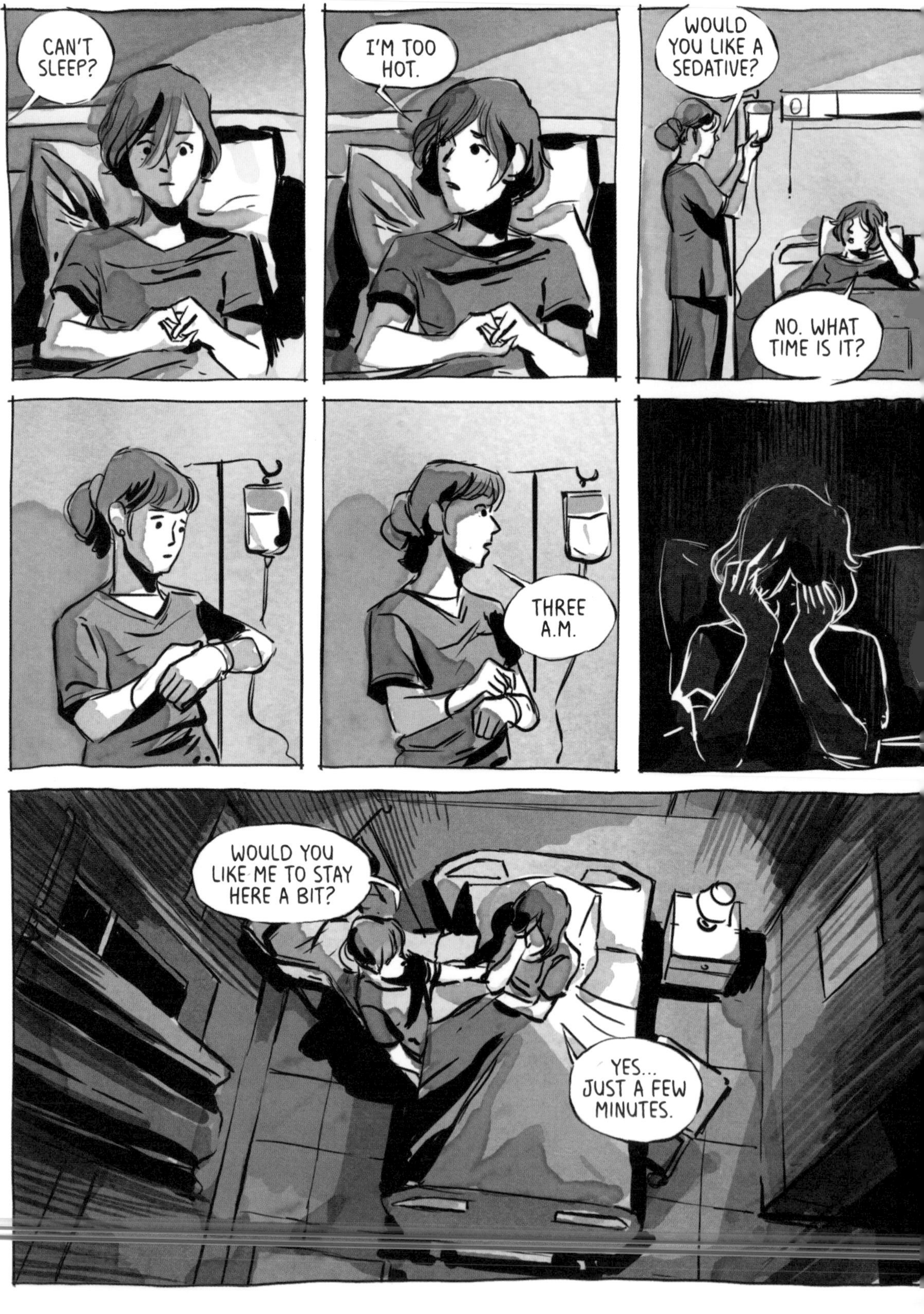
CAN'T SLEEP?
I'M TOO HOT.
WOULD YOU LIKE A SEDATIVE?
NO. WHAT TIME IS IT?
THREE A.M.
WOULD YOU LIKE ME TO STAY HERE A BIT?
YES... JUST A FEW MINUTES.

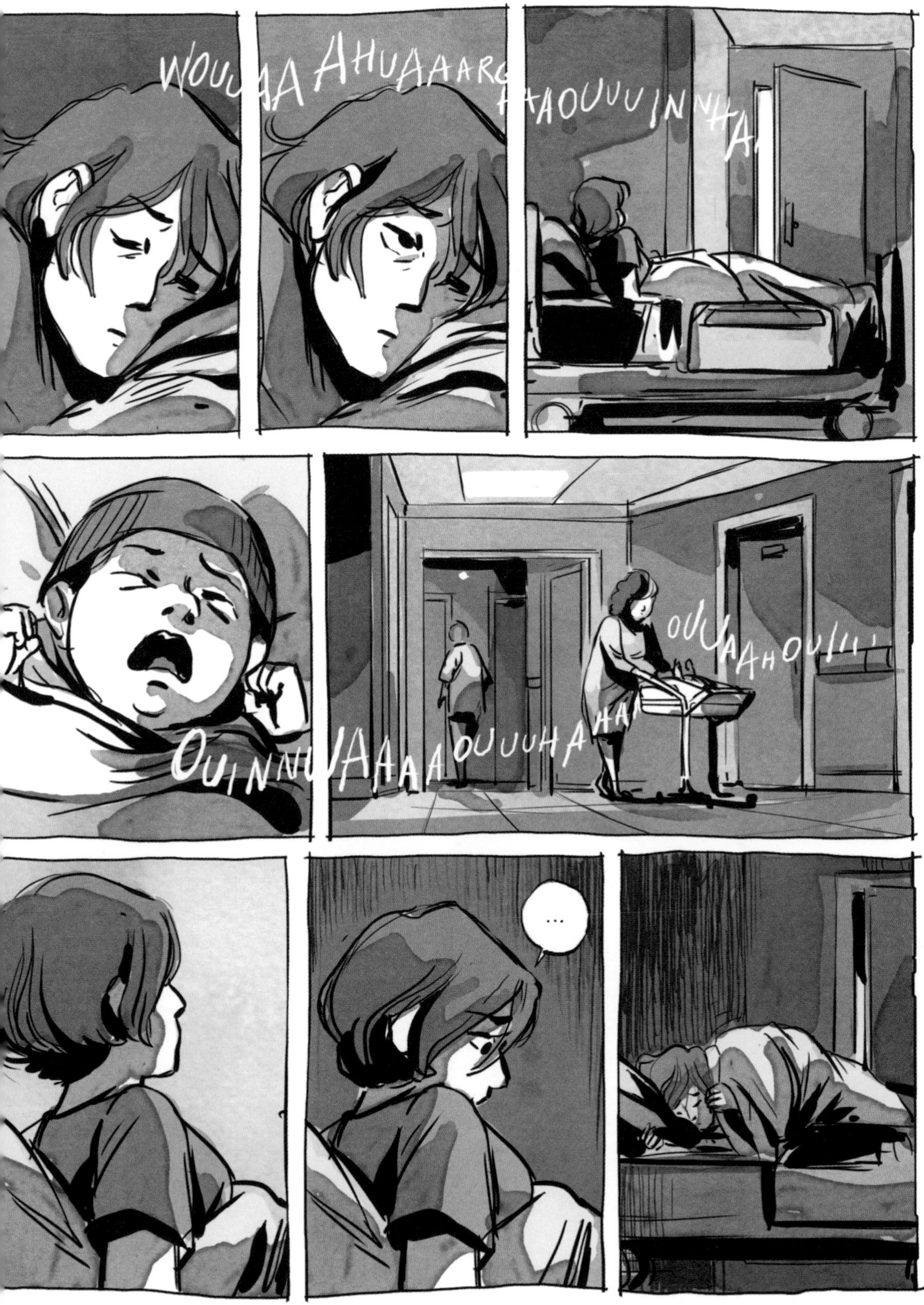

WOUUAA AHUAAARG
HAAOUUUINNHA
OUINNUAAAAOUUUHAHA
OUUAAHOUIII
...

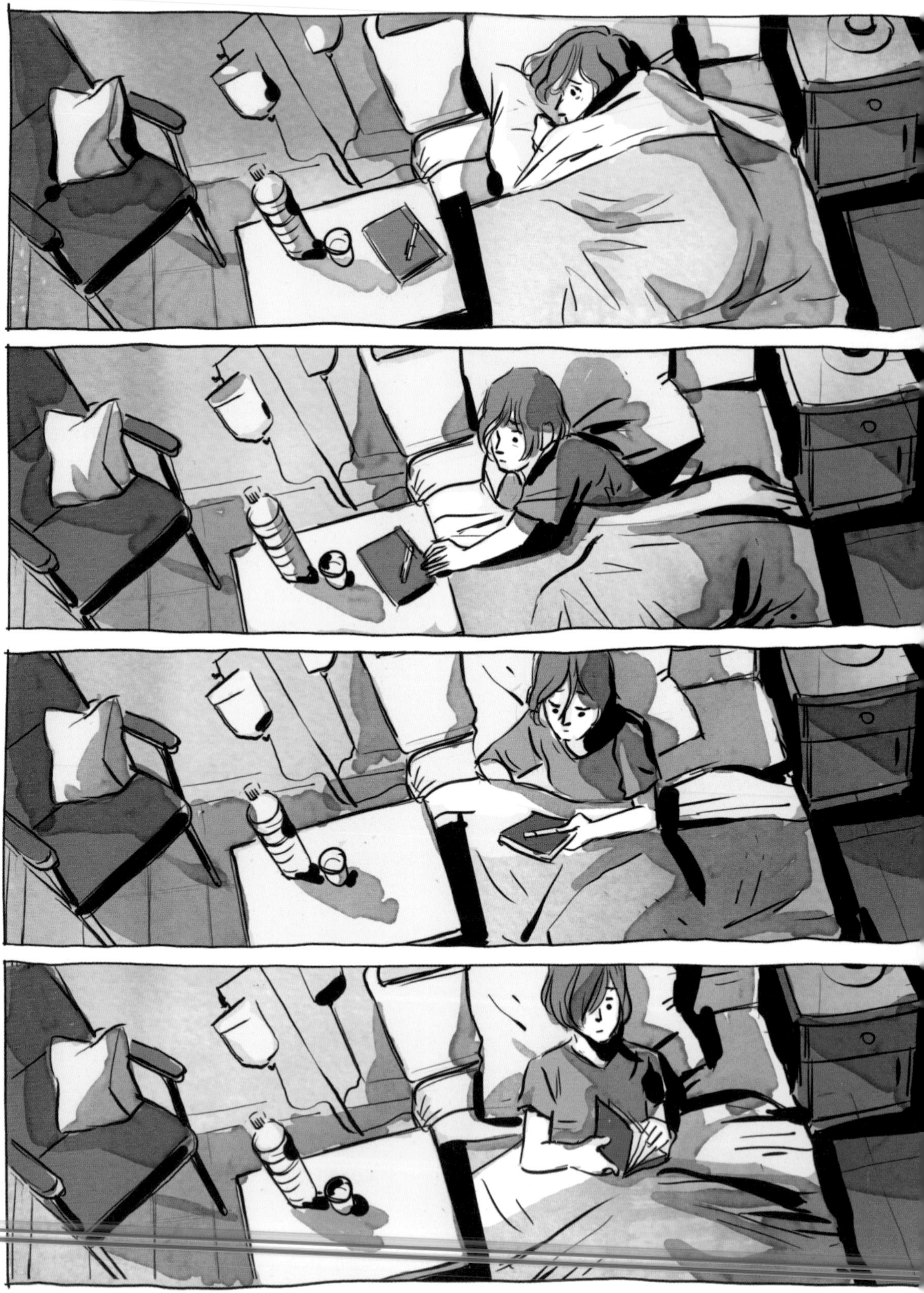

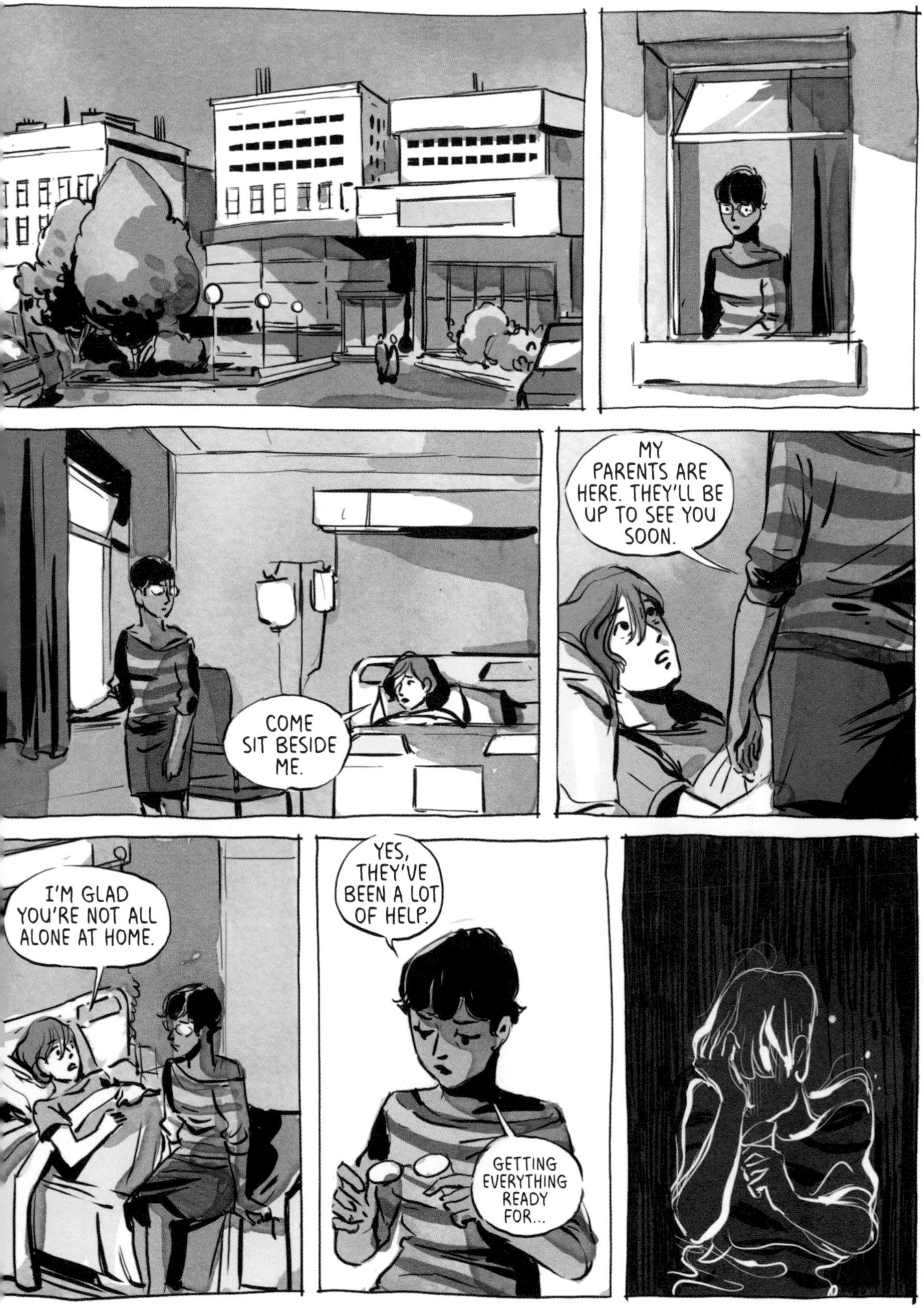
COME SIT BESIDE ME.
MY PARENTS ARE HERE. THEY'LL BE UP TO SEE YOU SOON.
I'M GLAD YOU'RE NOT ALL ALONE AT HOME.
YES, THEY'VE BEEN A LOT OF HELP.
GETTING EVERYTHING READY FOR...

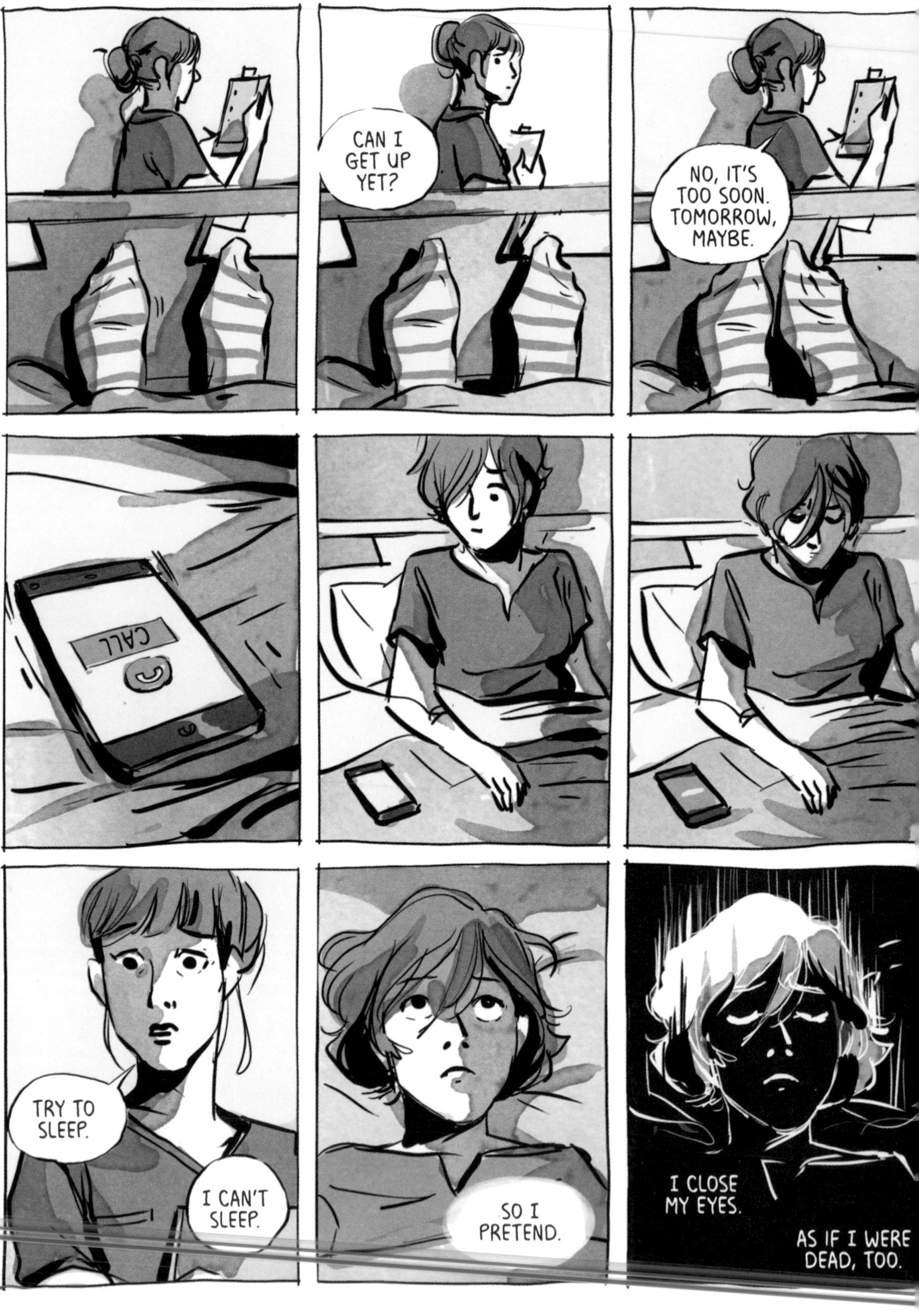
CAN I GET UP YET?
NO, IT'S TOO SOON. TOMORROW, MAYBE.
CALL
TRY TO SLEEP.
I CAN'T SLEEP.
SO I PRETEND.
I CLOSE MY EYES.
AS IF I WERE DEAD, TOO.

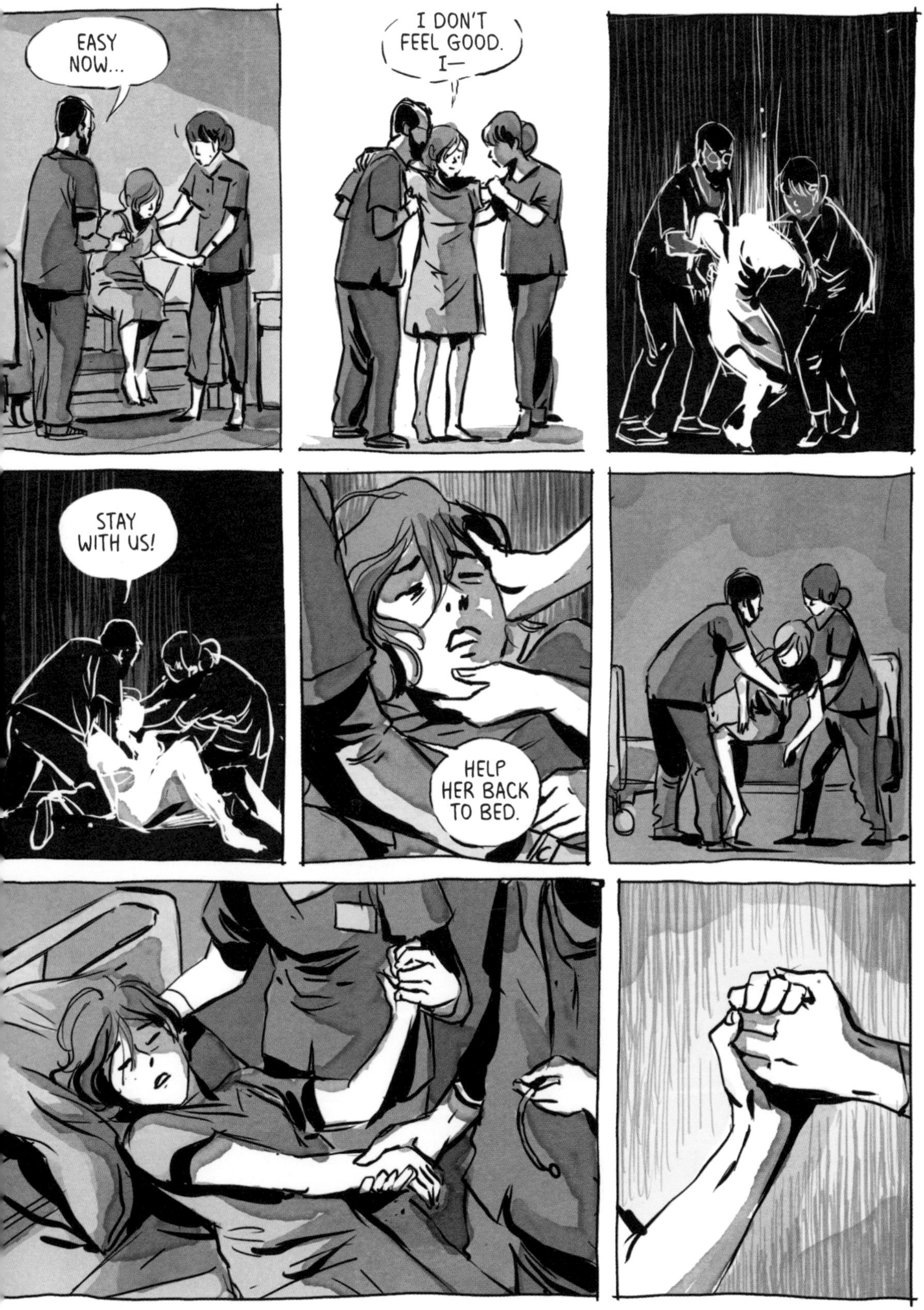
EASY NOW...
I DON'T FEEL GOOD. I—
STAY WITH US!
HELP HER BACK TO BED.

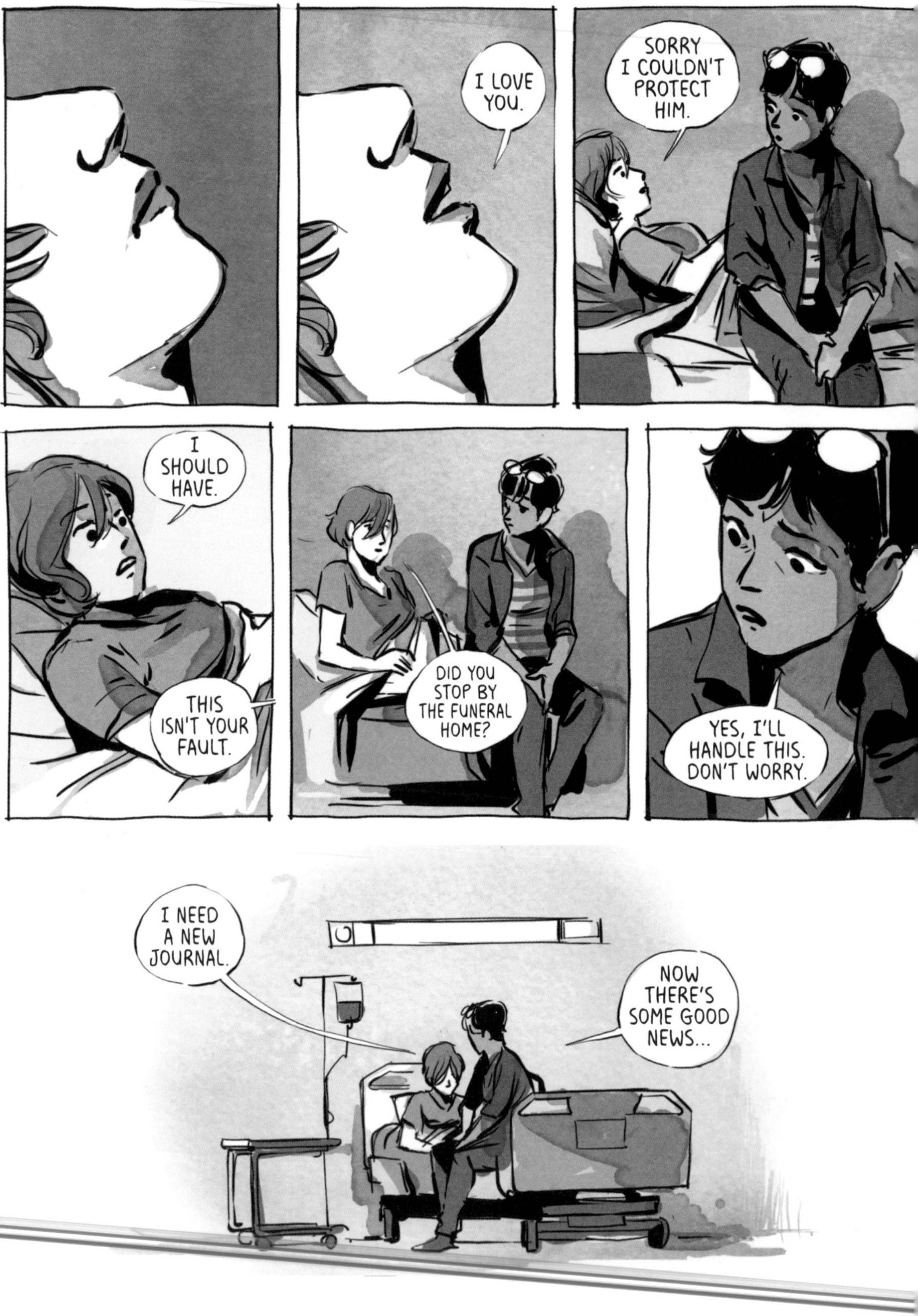
I LOVE YOU.
SORRY I COULDN'T PROTECT HIM.
I SHOULD HAVE.
THIS ISN'T YOUR FAULT.
DID YOU STOP BY THE FUNERAL HOME?
YES, I'LL HANDLE THIS. DON'T WORRY.
I NEED A NEW JOURNAL.
NOW THERE'S SOME GOOD NEWS...

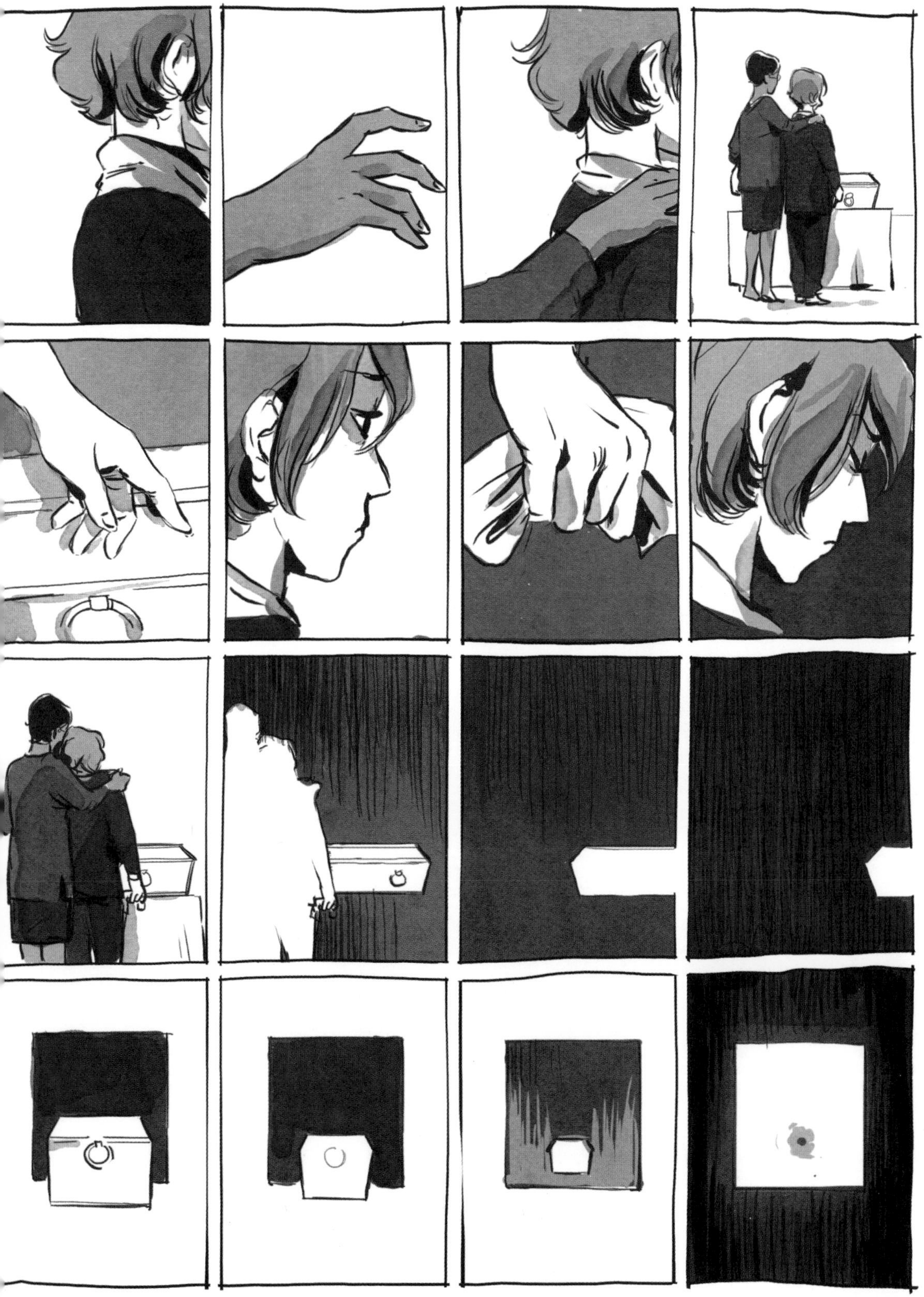

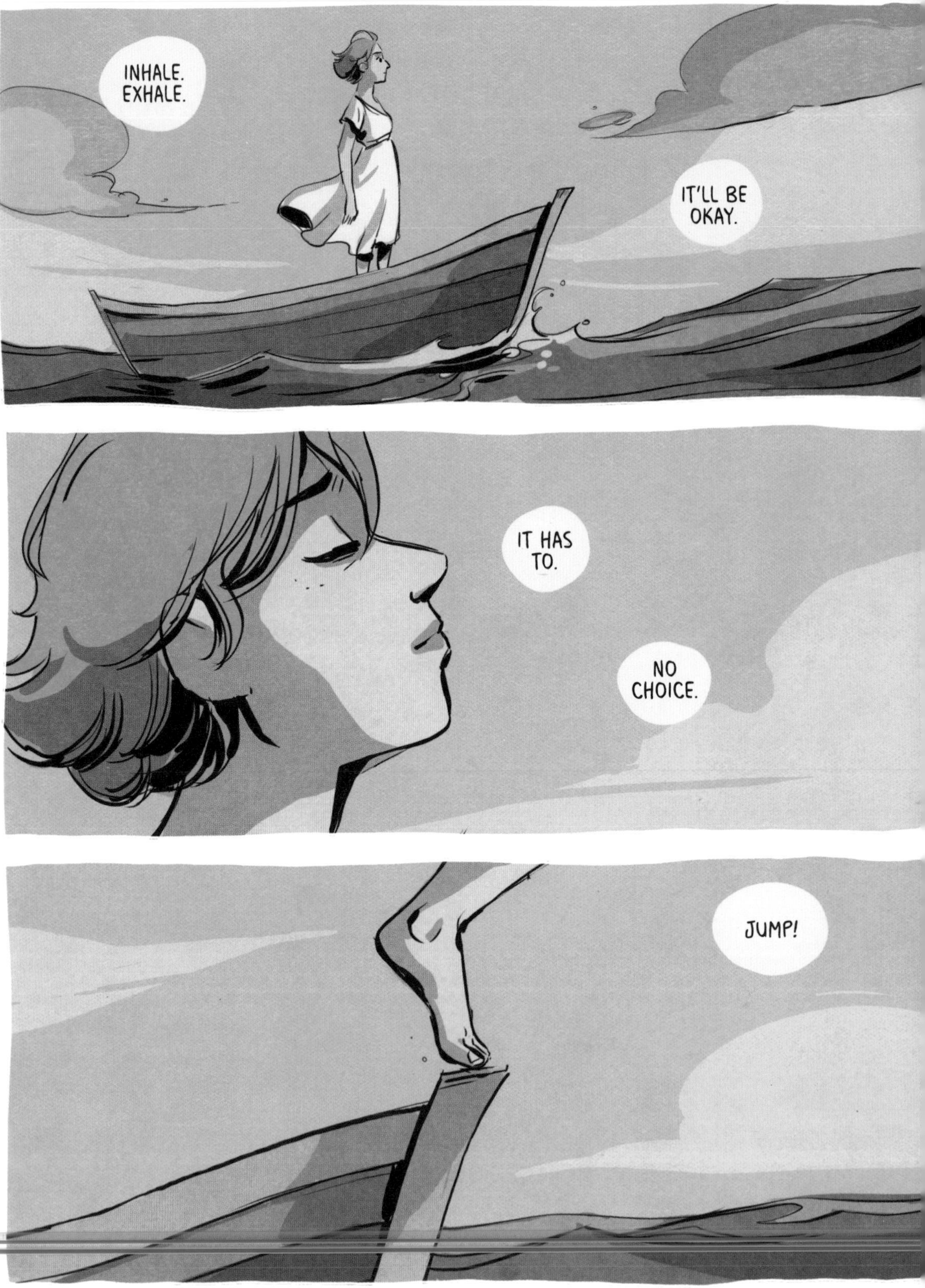
INHALE.
EXHALE.
IT'LL BE
OKAY.
IT HAS
TO.
NO
CHOICE.
JUMP!

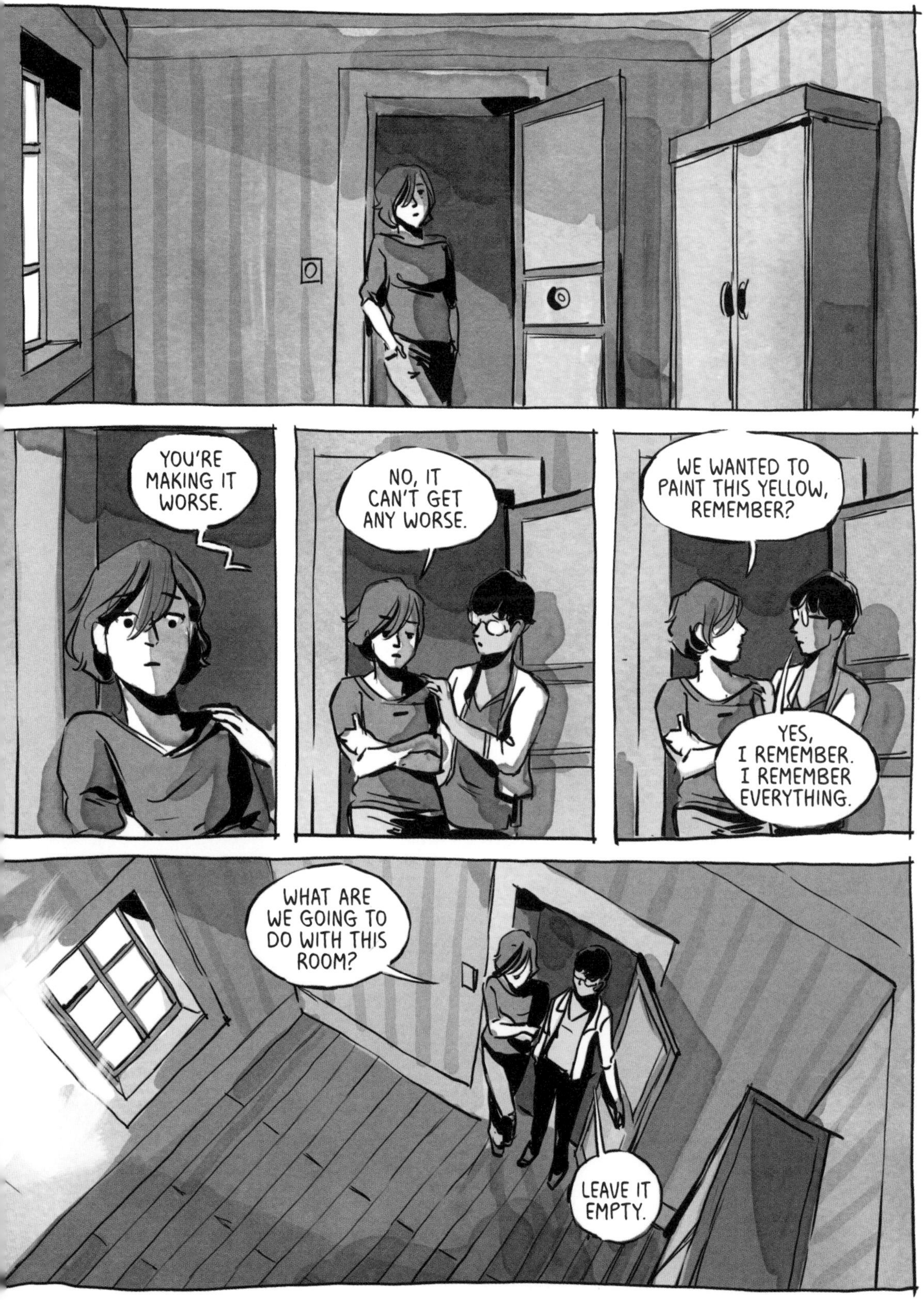
YOU'RE MAKING IT WORSE.
NO, IT CAN'T GET ANY WORSE.
WE WANTED TO PAINT THIS YELLOW, REMEMBER?
YES, I REMEMBER. I REMEMBER EVERYTHING.
WHAT ARE WE GOING TO DO WITH THIS ROOM?
LEAVE IT EMPTY.

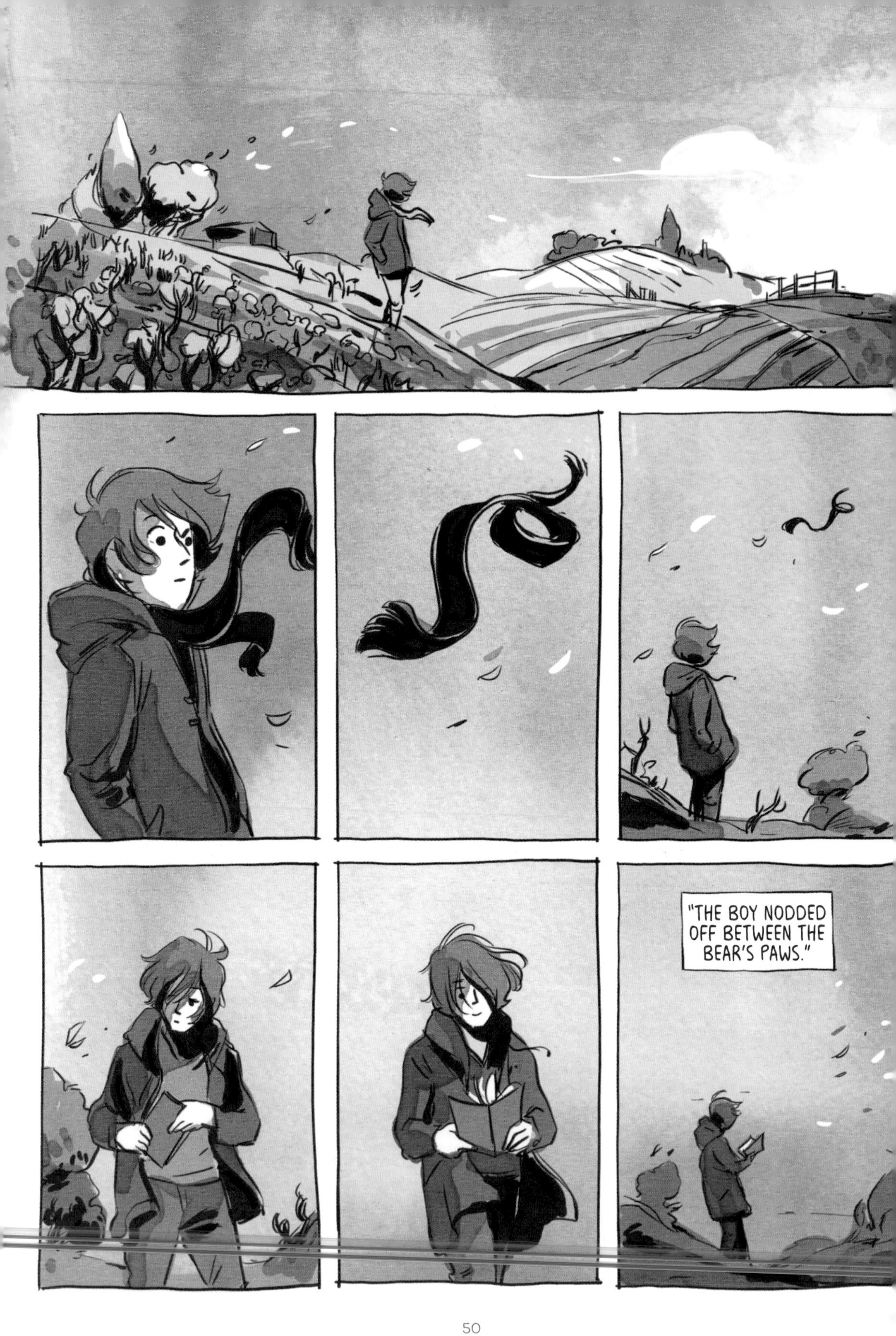
"THE BOY NODDED OFF BETWEEN THE BEAR'S PAWS."

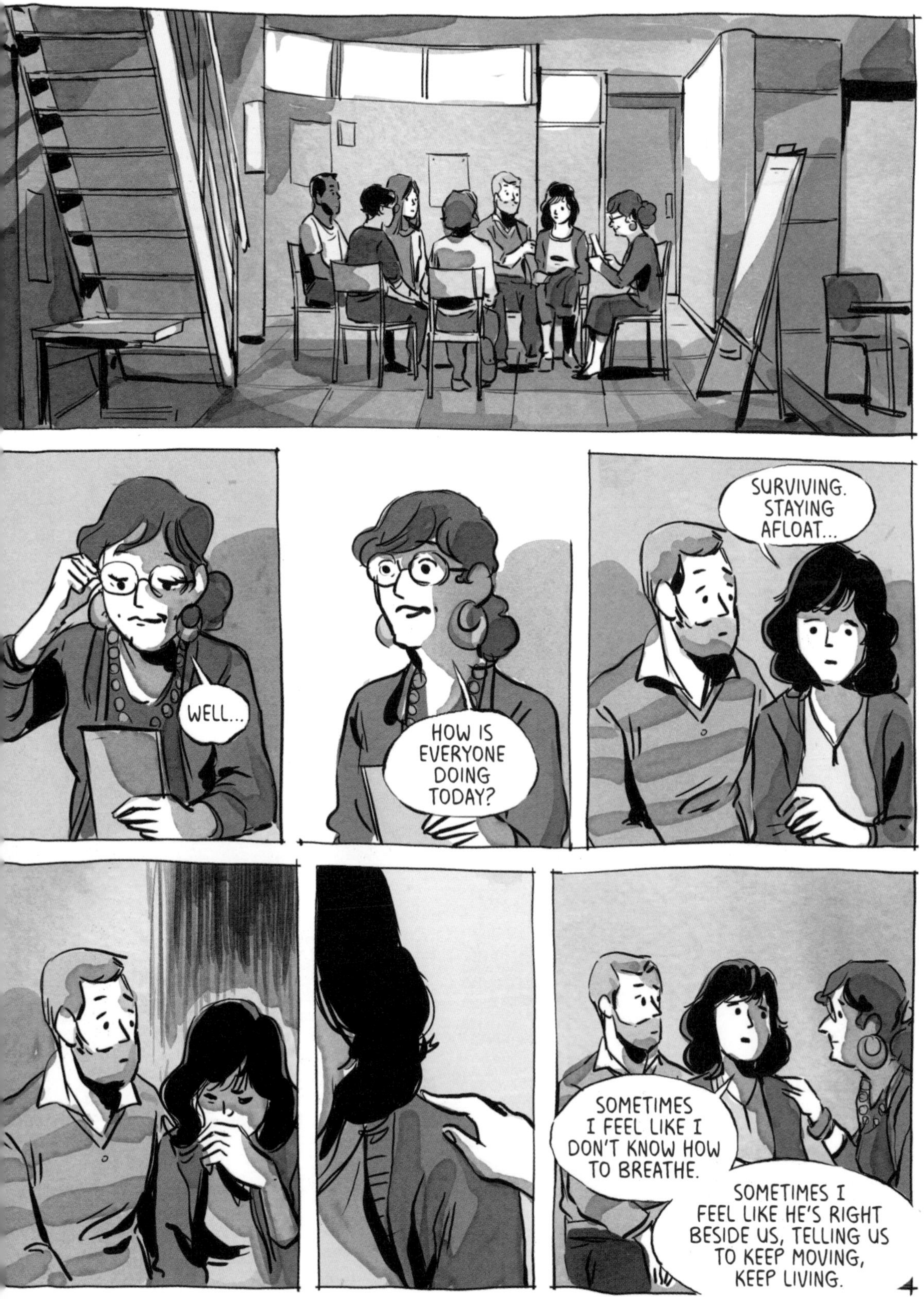
WELL...
HOW IS EVERYONE DOING TODAY?
SURVIVING. STAYING AFLOAT...
SOMETIMES I FEEL LIKE I DON'T KNOW HOW TO BREATHE.
SOMETIMES I FEEL LIKE HE'S RIGHT BESIDE US, TELLING US TO KEEP MOVING, KEEP LIVING.

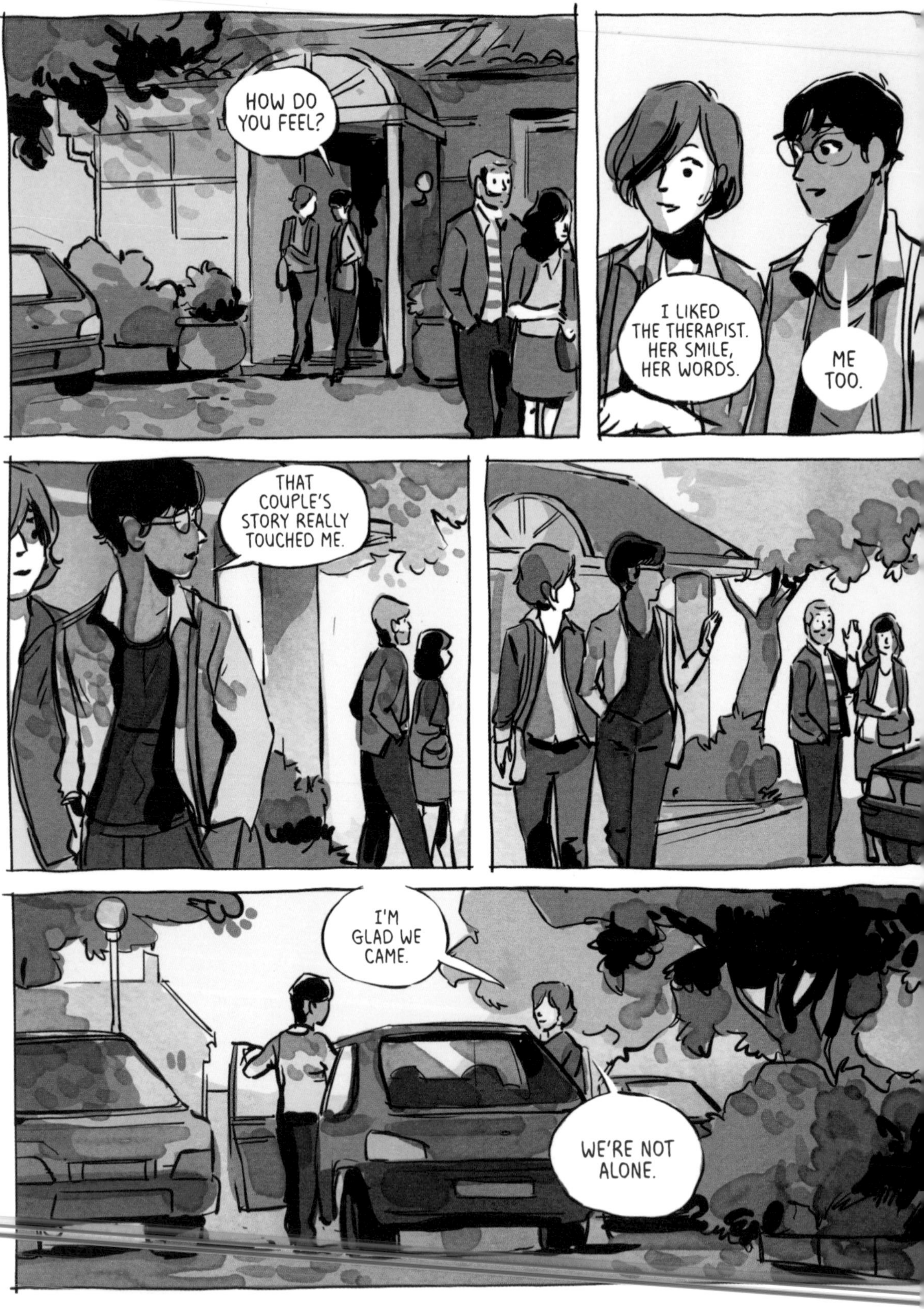
HOW DO YOU FEEL?
I LIKED THE THERAPIST. HER SMILE, HER WORDS.
ME TOO.
THAT COUPLE'S STORY REALLY TOUCHED ME.
I'M GLAD WE CAME.
WE'RE NOT ALONE.

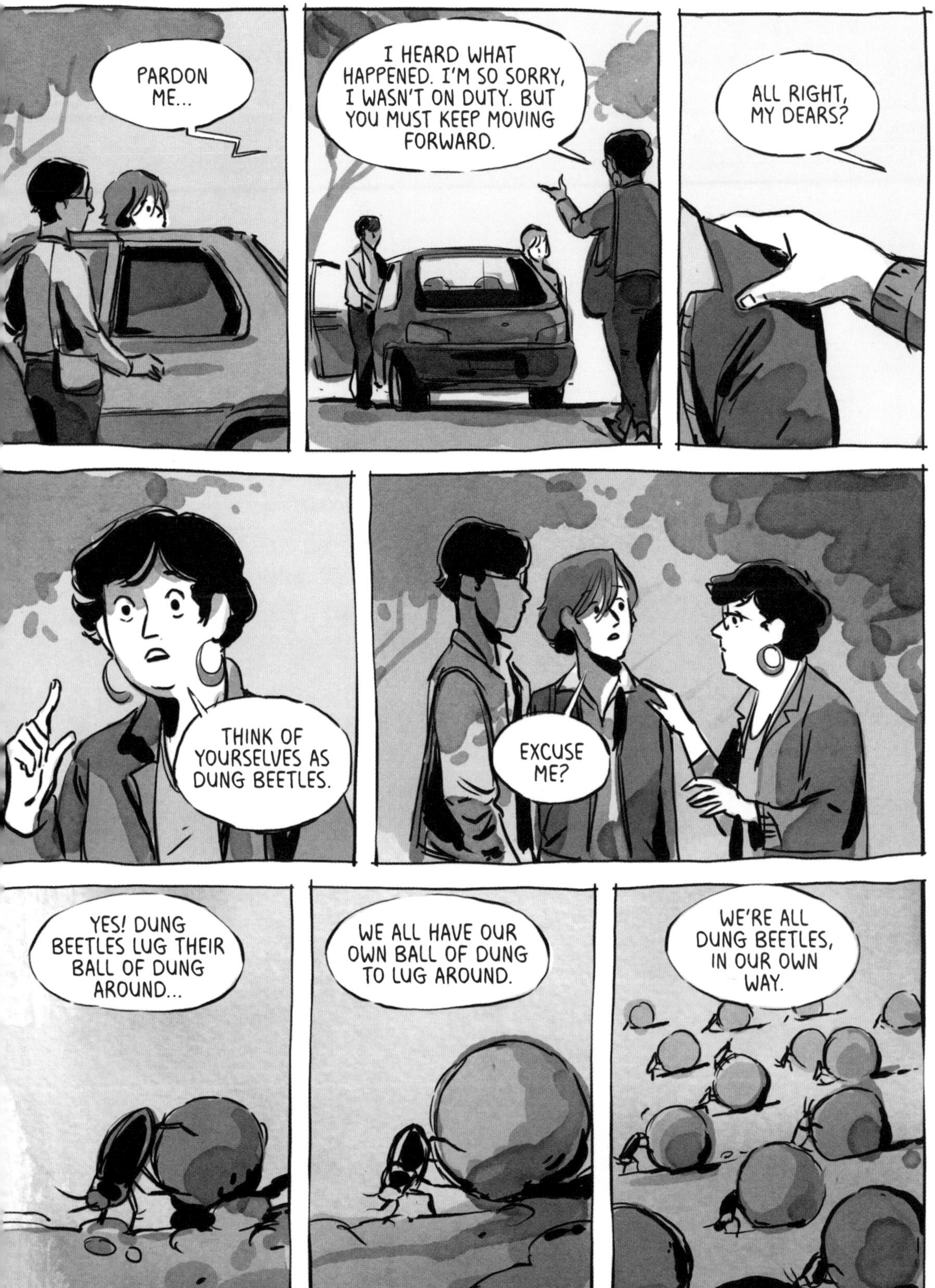
PARDON ME...
I HEARD WHAT HAPPENED. I'M SO SORRY, I WASN'T ON DUTY. BUT YOU MUST KEEP MOVING FORWARD.
ALL RIGHT, MY DEARS?
THINK OF YOURSELVES AS DUNG BEETLES.
EXCUSE ME?
YES! DUNG BEETLES LUG THEIR BALL OF DUNG AROUND...
WE ALL HAVE OUR OWN BALL OF DUNG TO LUG AROUND.
WE'RE ALL DUNG BEETLES, IN OUR OWN WAY.

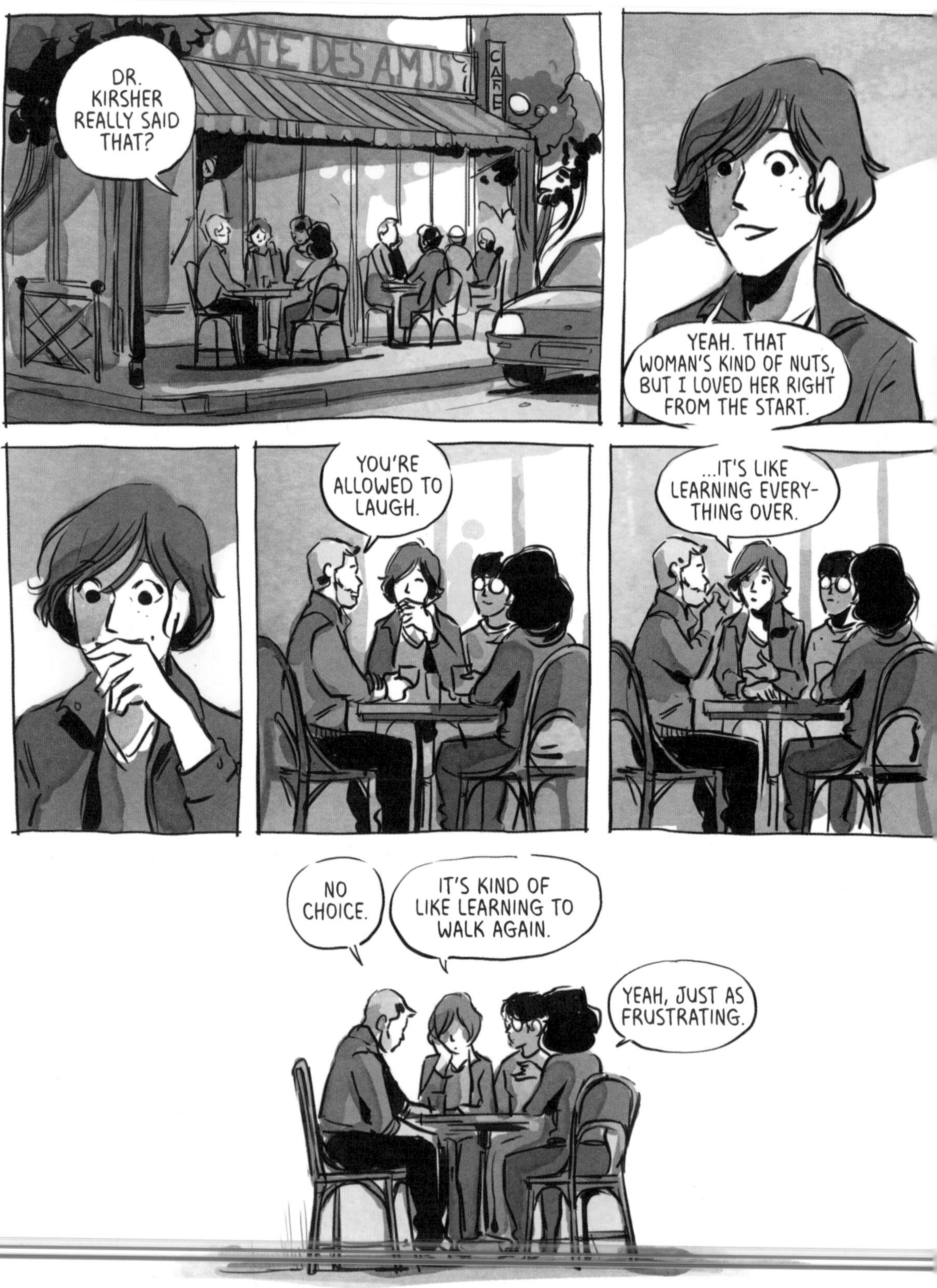
CAFE DES AMIS
CAFE
DR. KIRSHER REALLY SAID THAT?
YEAH. THAT WOMAN'S KIND OF NUTS, BUT I LOVED HER RIGHT FROM THE START.
YOU'RE ALLOWED TO LAUGH.
...IT'S LIKE LEARNING EVERY-THING OVER.
NO CHOICE.
IT'S KIND OF LIKE LEARNING TO WALK AGAIN.
YEAH, JUST AS FRUSTRATING.

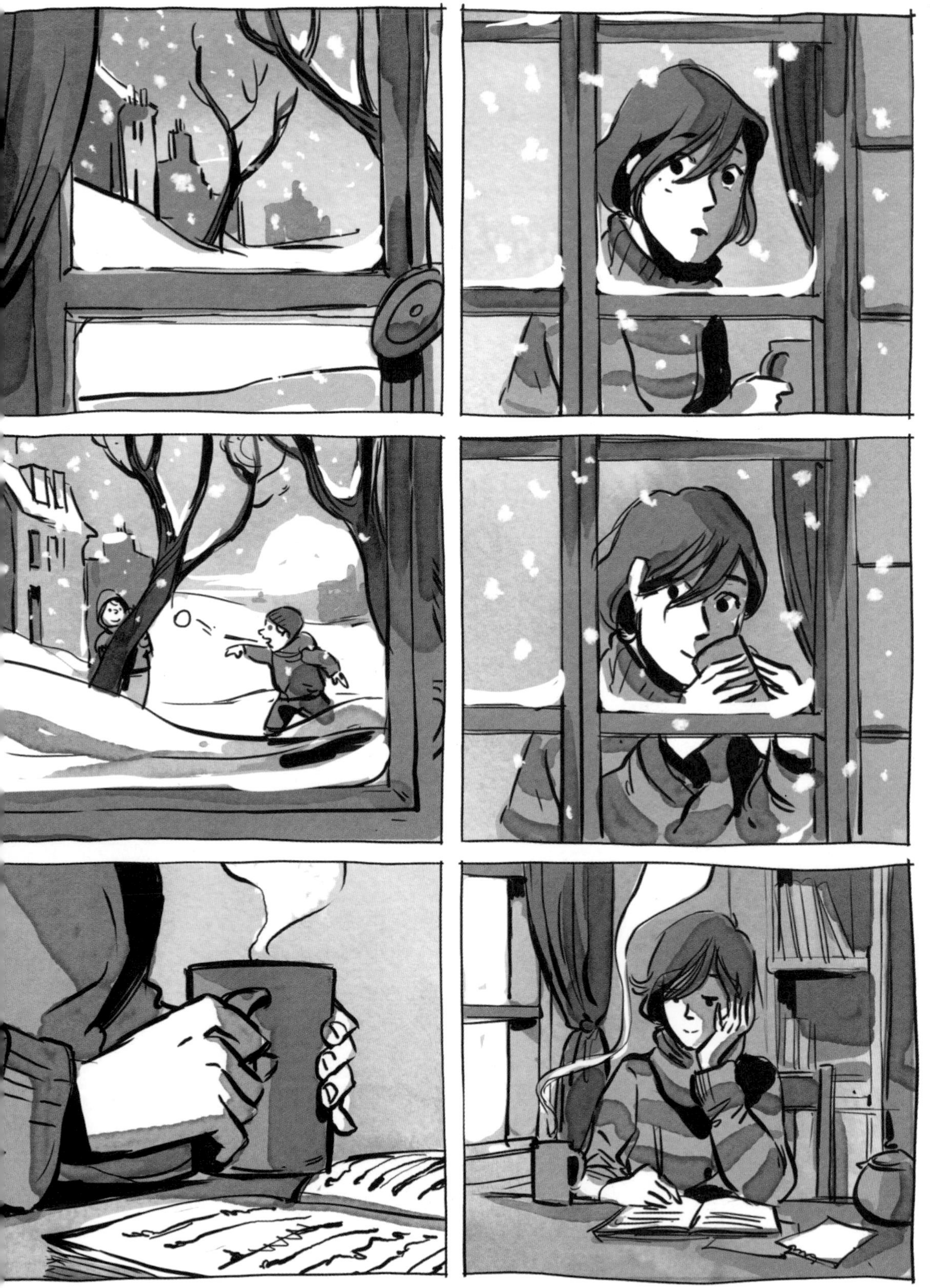

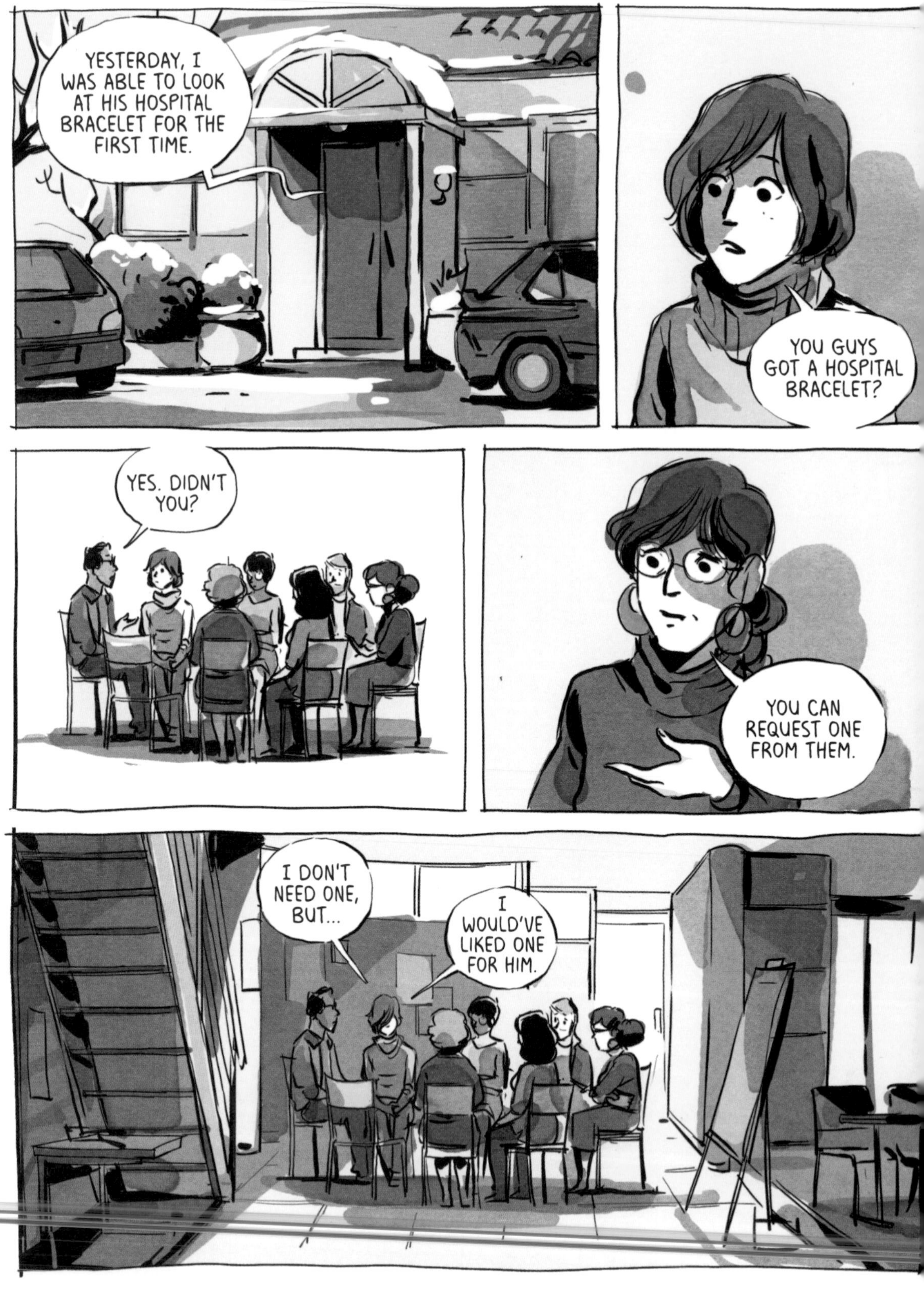
YESTERDAY, I WAS ABLE TO LOOK AT HIS HOSPITAL BRACELET FOR THE FIRST TIME.
YOU GUYS GOT A HOSPITAL BRACELET?
YES. DIDN'T YOU?
YOU CAN REQUEST ONE FROM THEM.
I DON'T NEED ONE, BUT...
I WOULD'VE LIKED ONE FOR HIM.

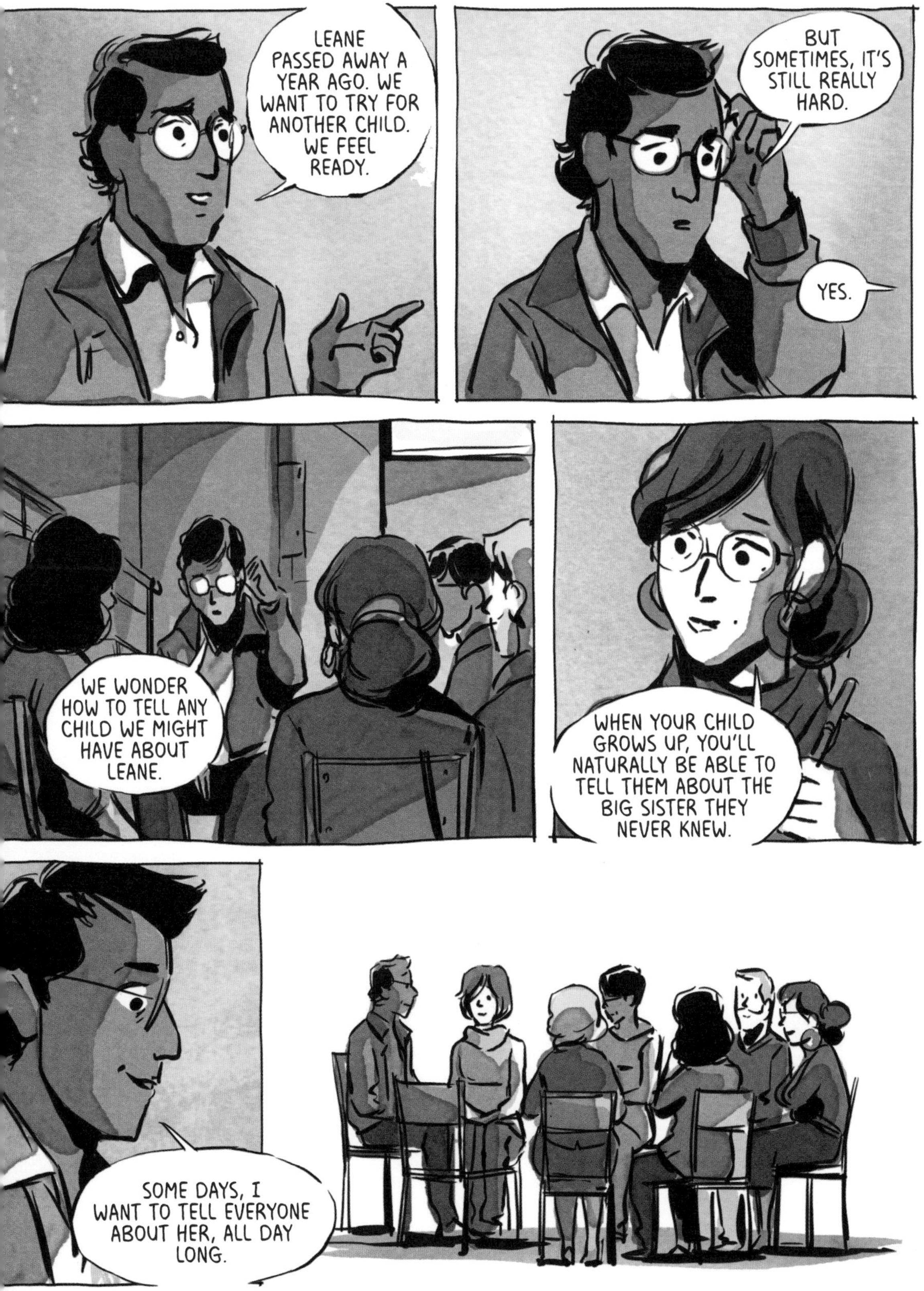
LEANE PASSED AWAY A YEAR AGO. WE WANT TO TRY FOR ANOTHER CHILD. WE FEEL READY.
BUT SOMETIMES, IT'S STILL REALLY HARD.
YES.
WE WONDER HOW TO TELL ANY CHILD WE MIGHT HAVE ABOUT LEANE.
WHEN YOUR CHILD GROWS UP, YOU'LL NATURALLY BE ABLE TO TELL THEM ABOUT THE BIG SISTER THEY NEVER KNEW.
SOME DAYS, I WANT TO TELL EVERYONE ABOUT HER, ALL DAY LONG.

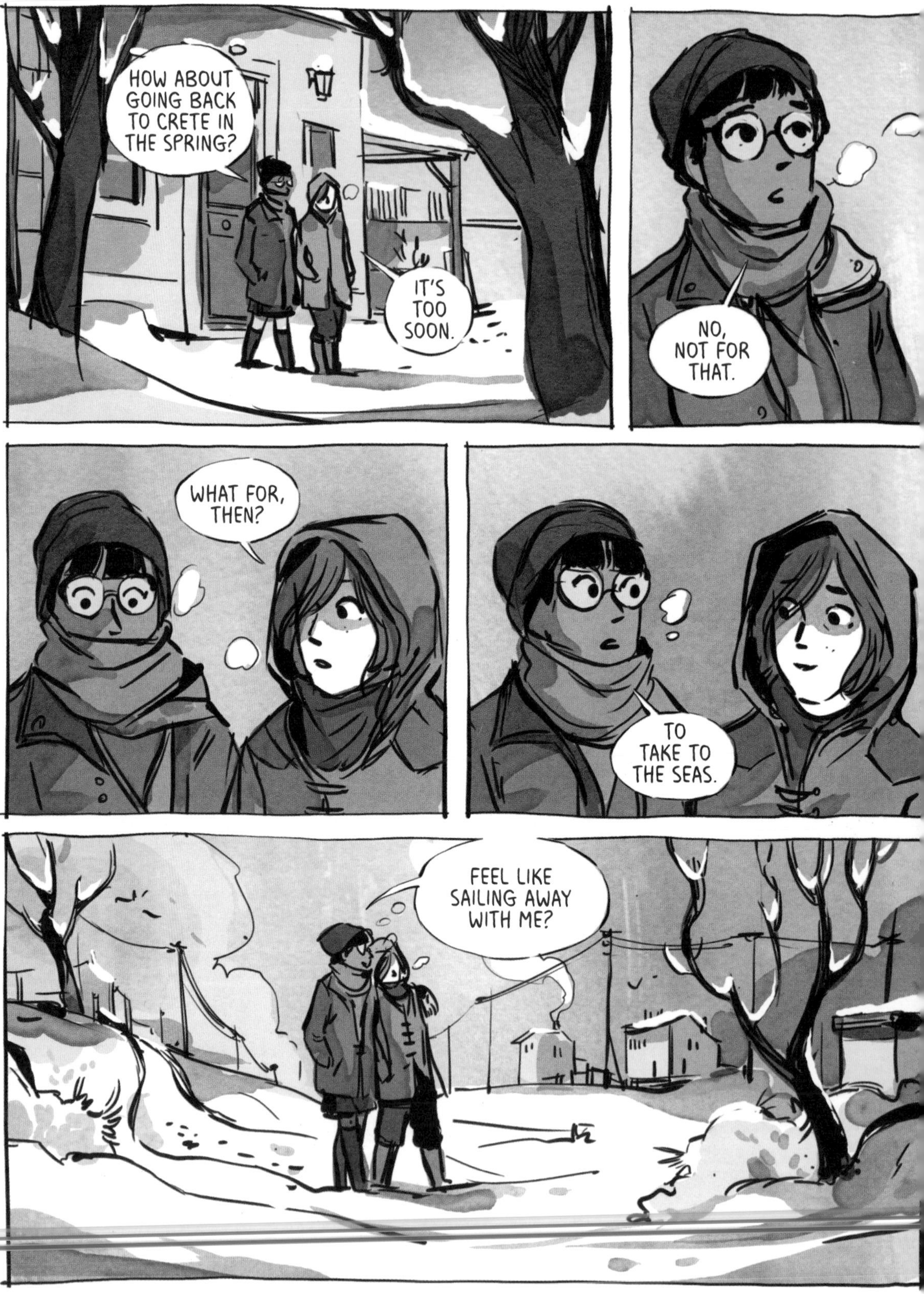
HOW ABOUT GOING BACK TO CRETE IN THE SPRING?
IT'S TOO SOON.
NO, NOT FOR THAT.
WHAT FOR, THEN?
TO TAKE TO THE SEAS.
FEEL LIKE SAILING AWAY WITH ME?

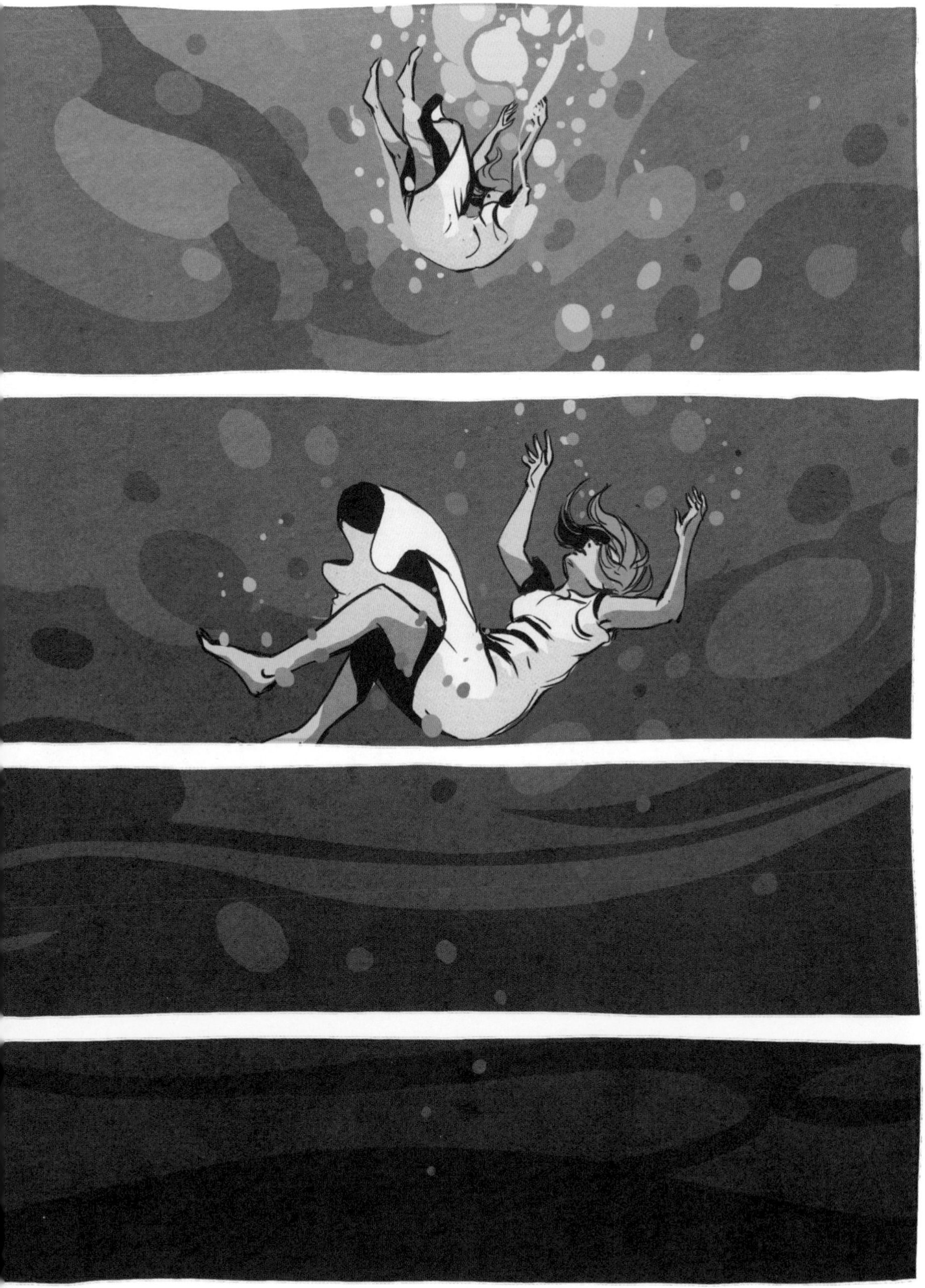

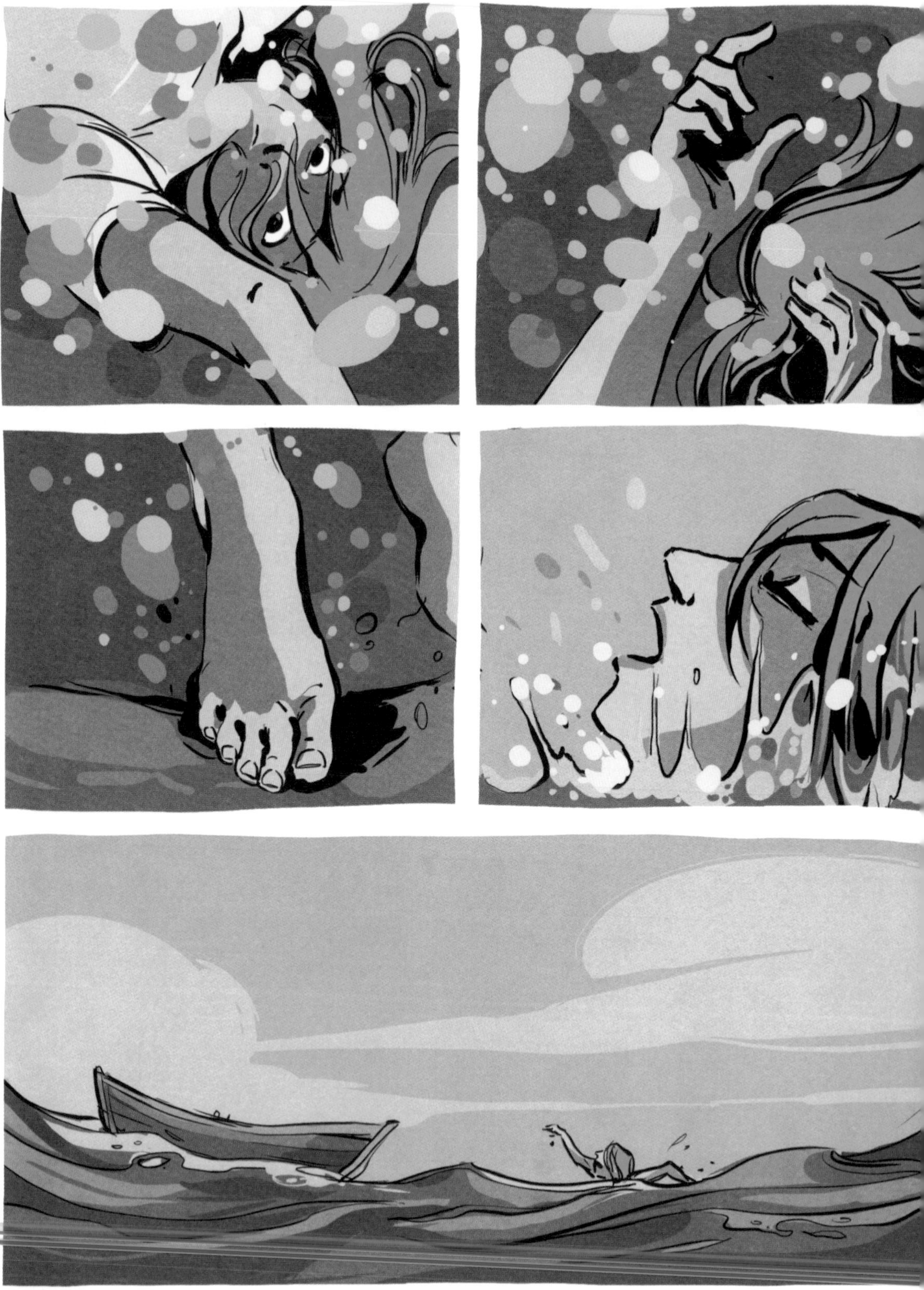

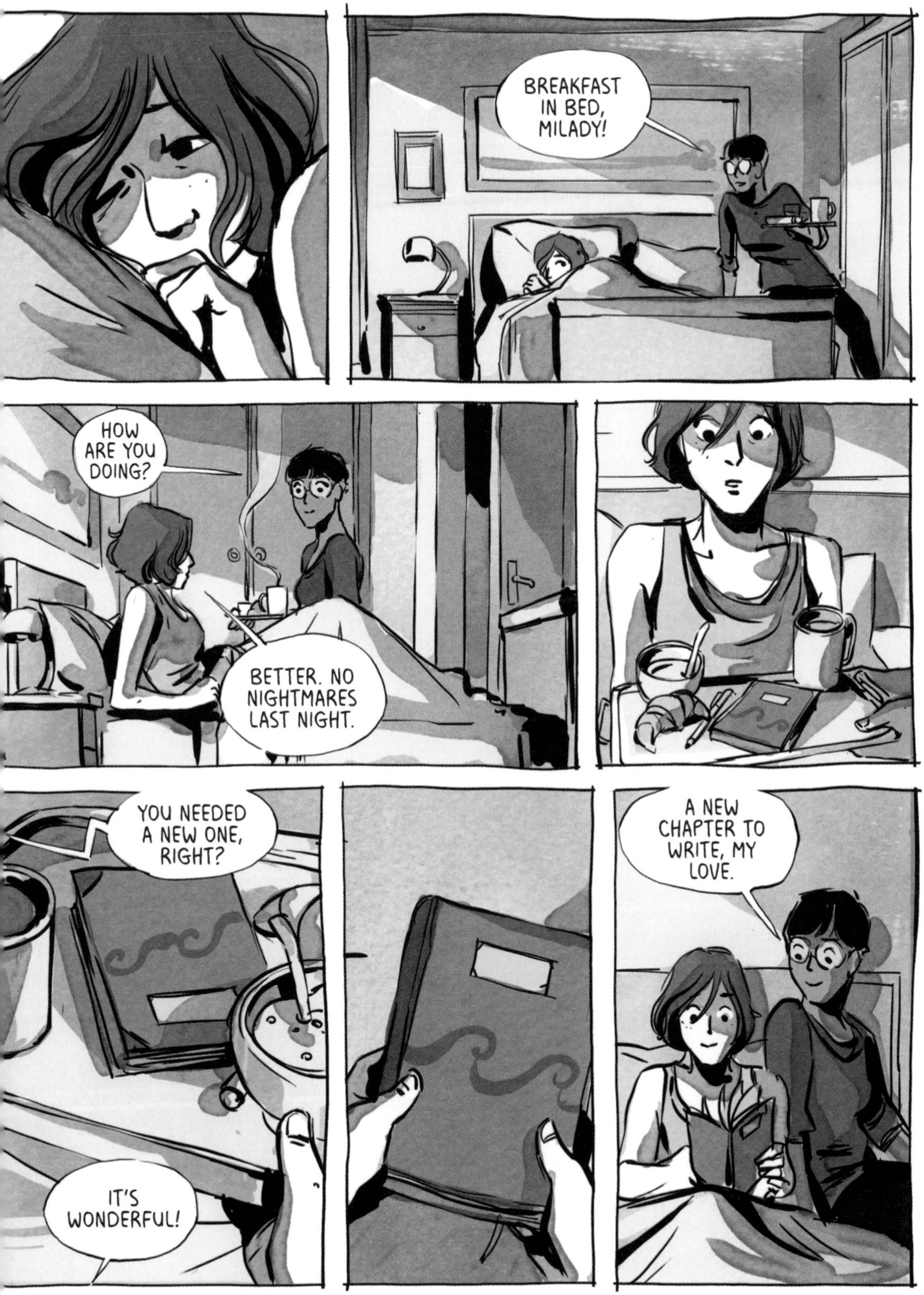
BREAKFAST IN BED, MILADY!
HOW ARE YOU DOING?
BETTER. NO NIGHTMARES LAST NIGHT.
YOU NEEDED A NEW ONE, RIGHT?
IT'S WONDERFUL!
A NEW CHAPTER TO WRITE, MY LOVE.

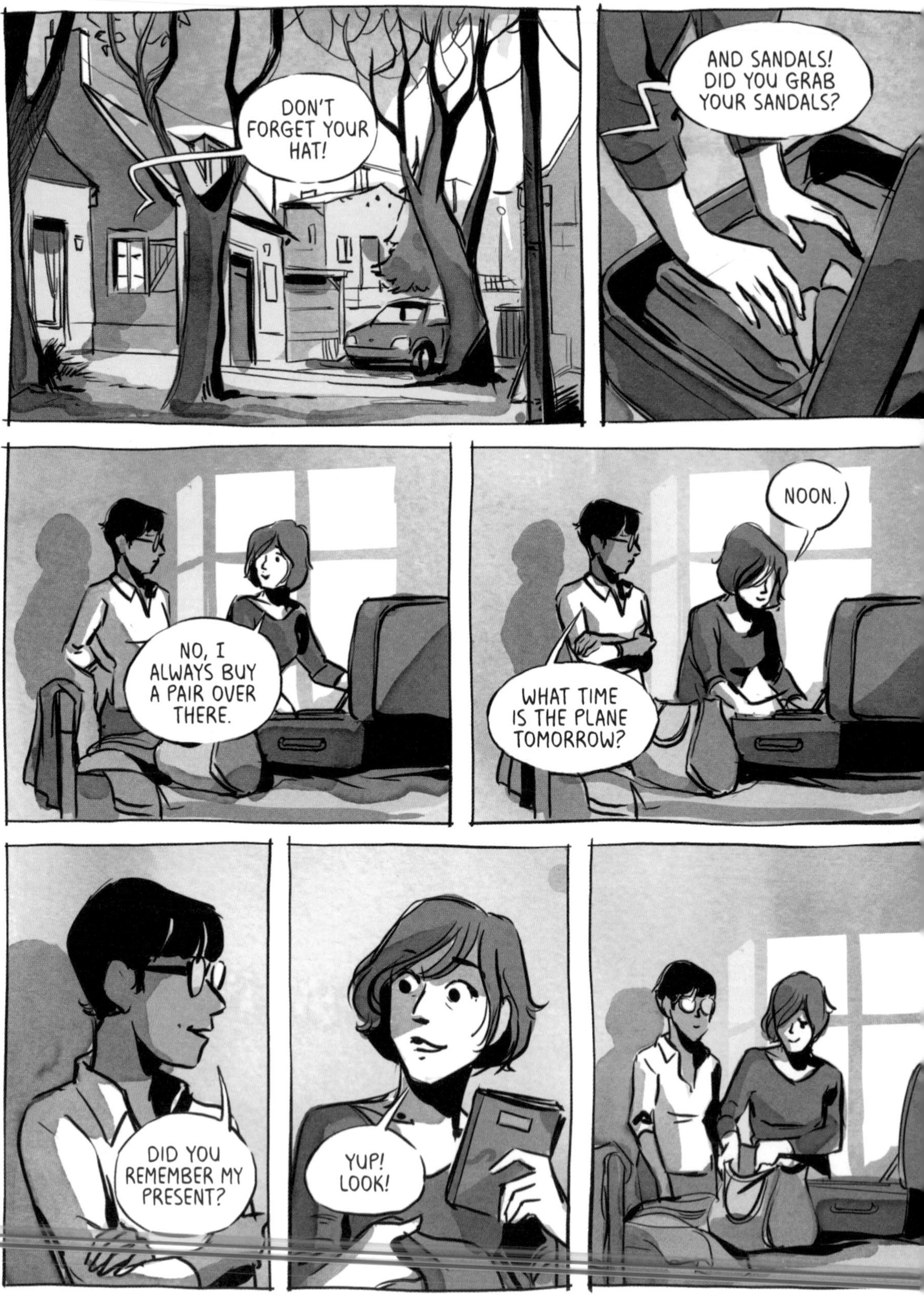
DON'T FORGET YOUR HAT!
AND SANDALS! DID YOU GRAB YOUR SANDALS?
NO, I ALWAYS BUY A PAIR OVER THERE.
WHAT TIME IS THE PLANE TOMORROW?
NOON.
DID YOU REMEMBER MY PRESENT?
YUP! LOOK!

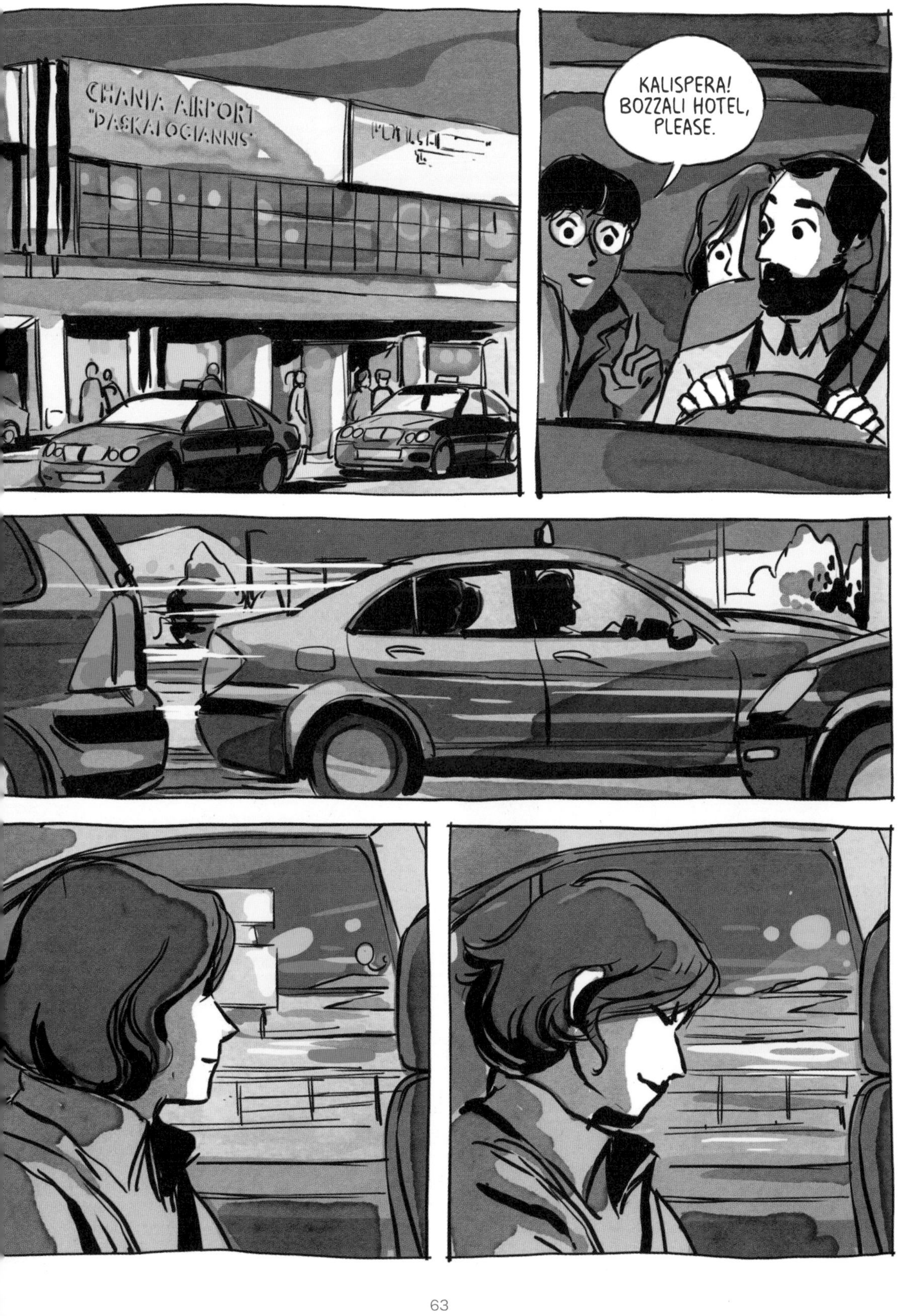
CHANIA AIRPORT
"DASKALOGIANNIS"
KALISPERA! BOZZALI HOTEL, PLEASE.

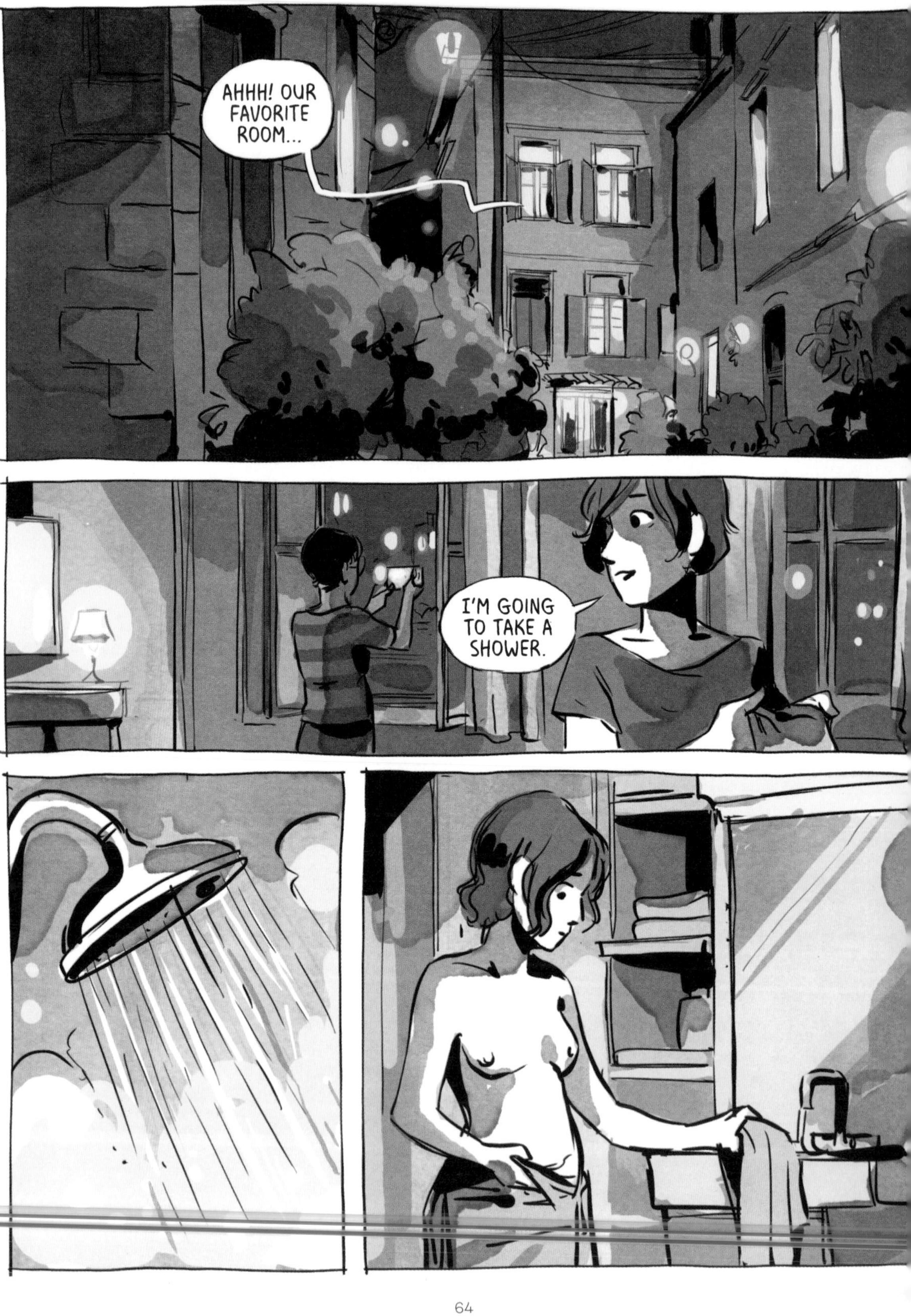
AHHH! OUR FAVORITE ROOM...
I'M GOING TO TAKE A SHOWER.

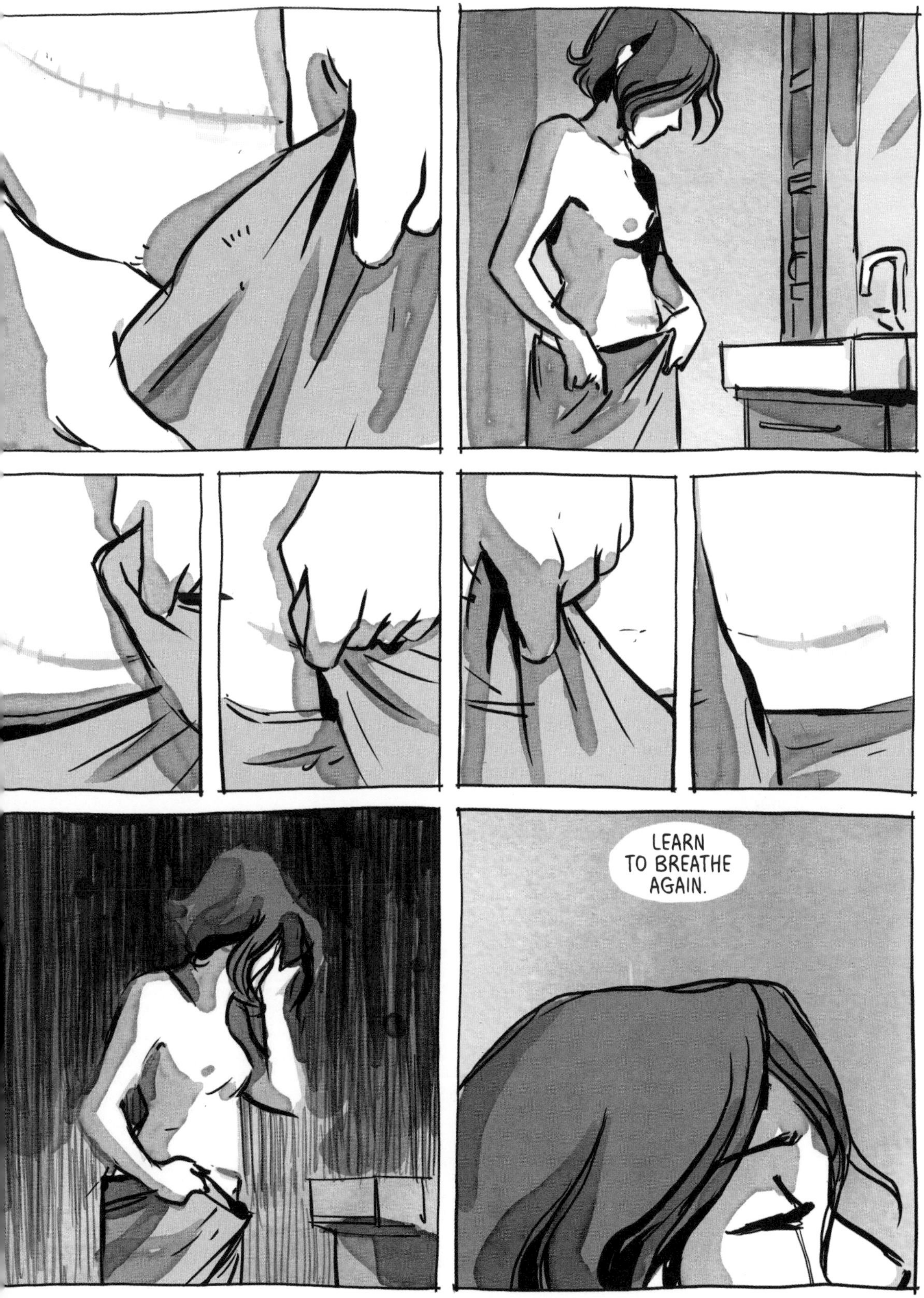
LEARN TO BREATHE AGAIN.

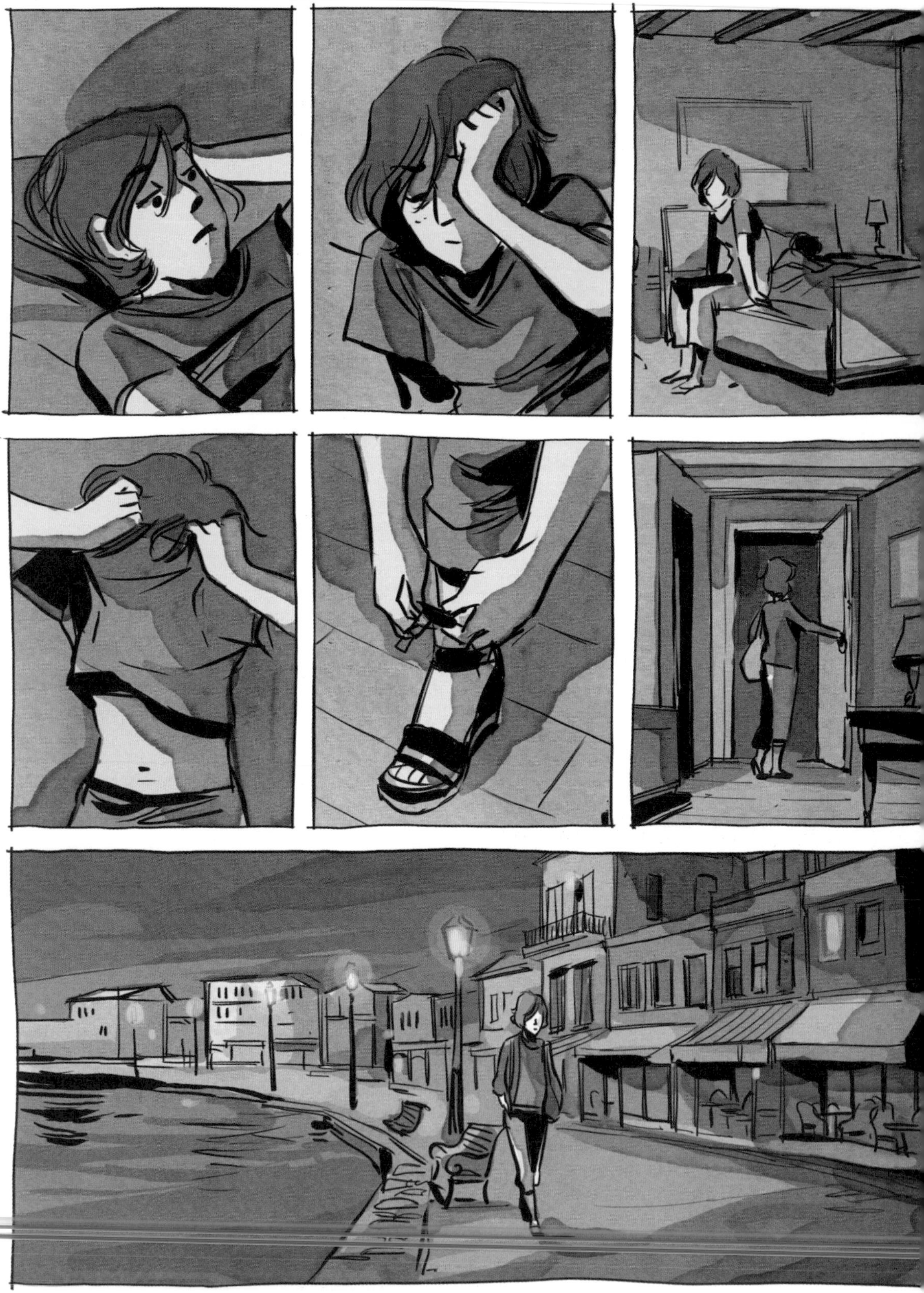

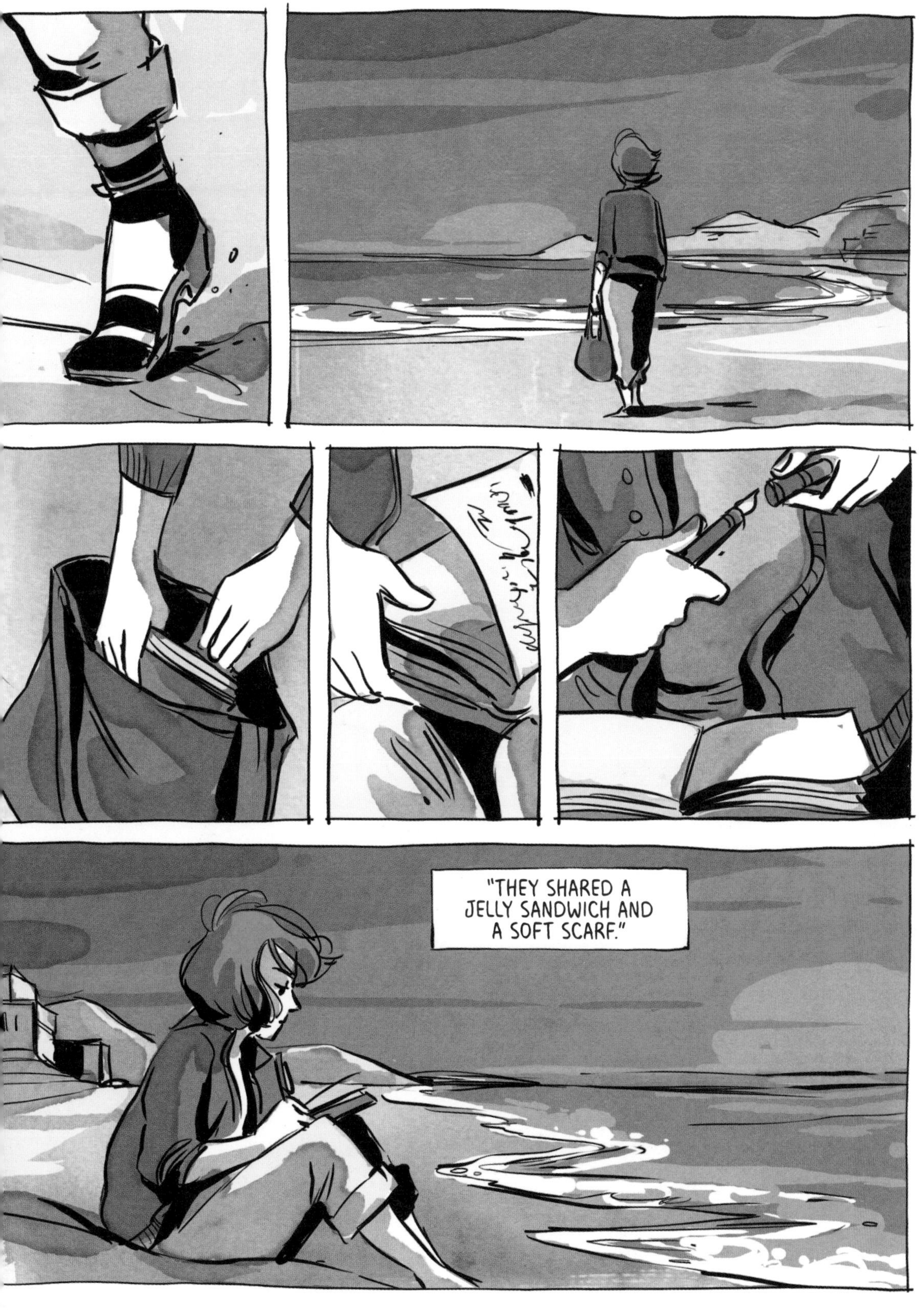
"THEY SHARED A
JELLY SANDWICH AND
A SOFT SCARF."

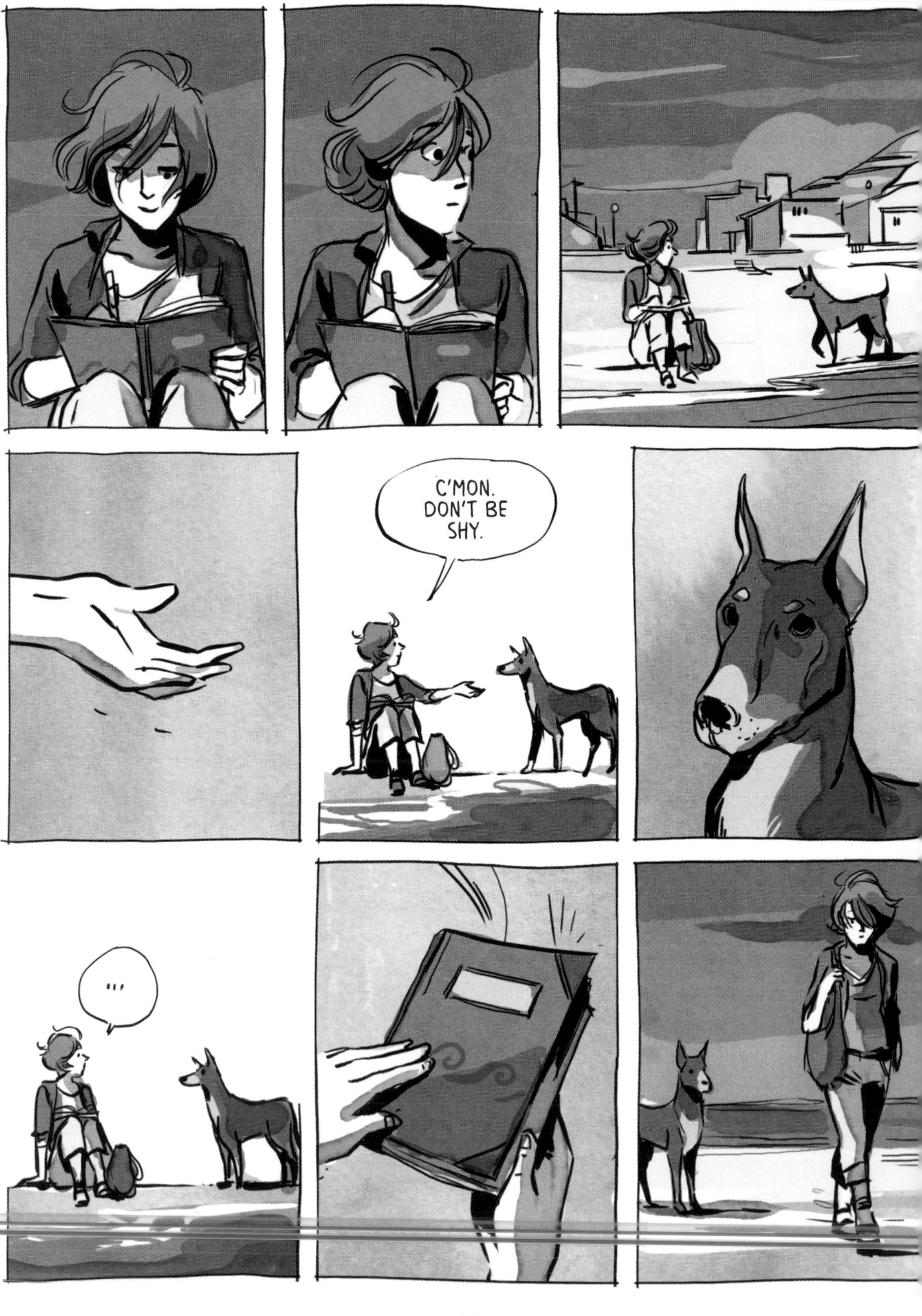
C'MON. DON'T BE SHY.
...

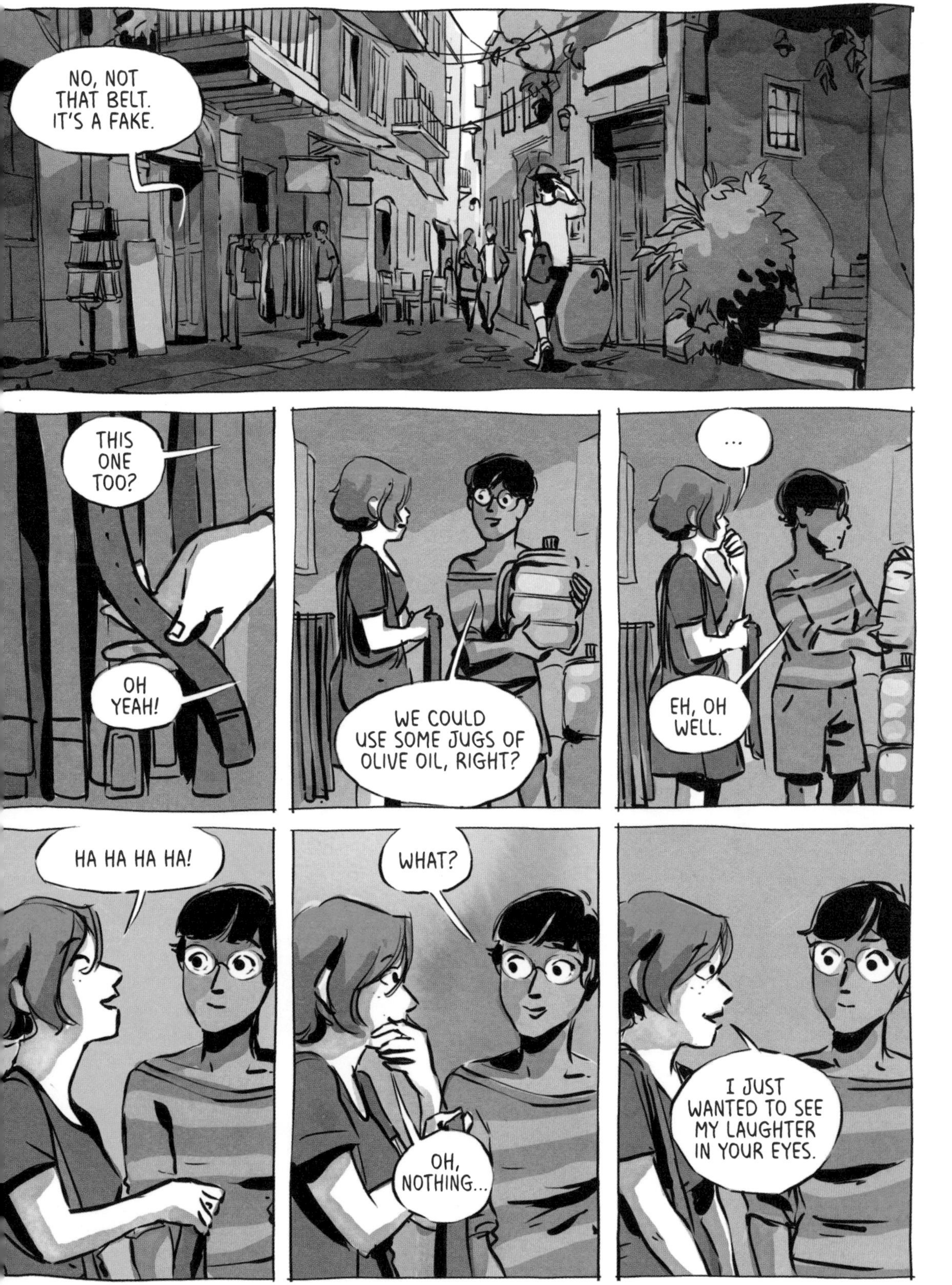
NO, NOT THAT BELT. IT'S A FAKE.
THIS ONE TOO?
OH YEAH!
WE COULD USE SOME JUGS OF OLIVE OIL, RIGHT?
...
EH, OH WELL.
HA HA HA HA!
WHAT?
OH, NOTHING...
I JUST WANTED TO SEE MY LAUGHTER IN YOUR EYES.

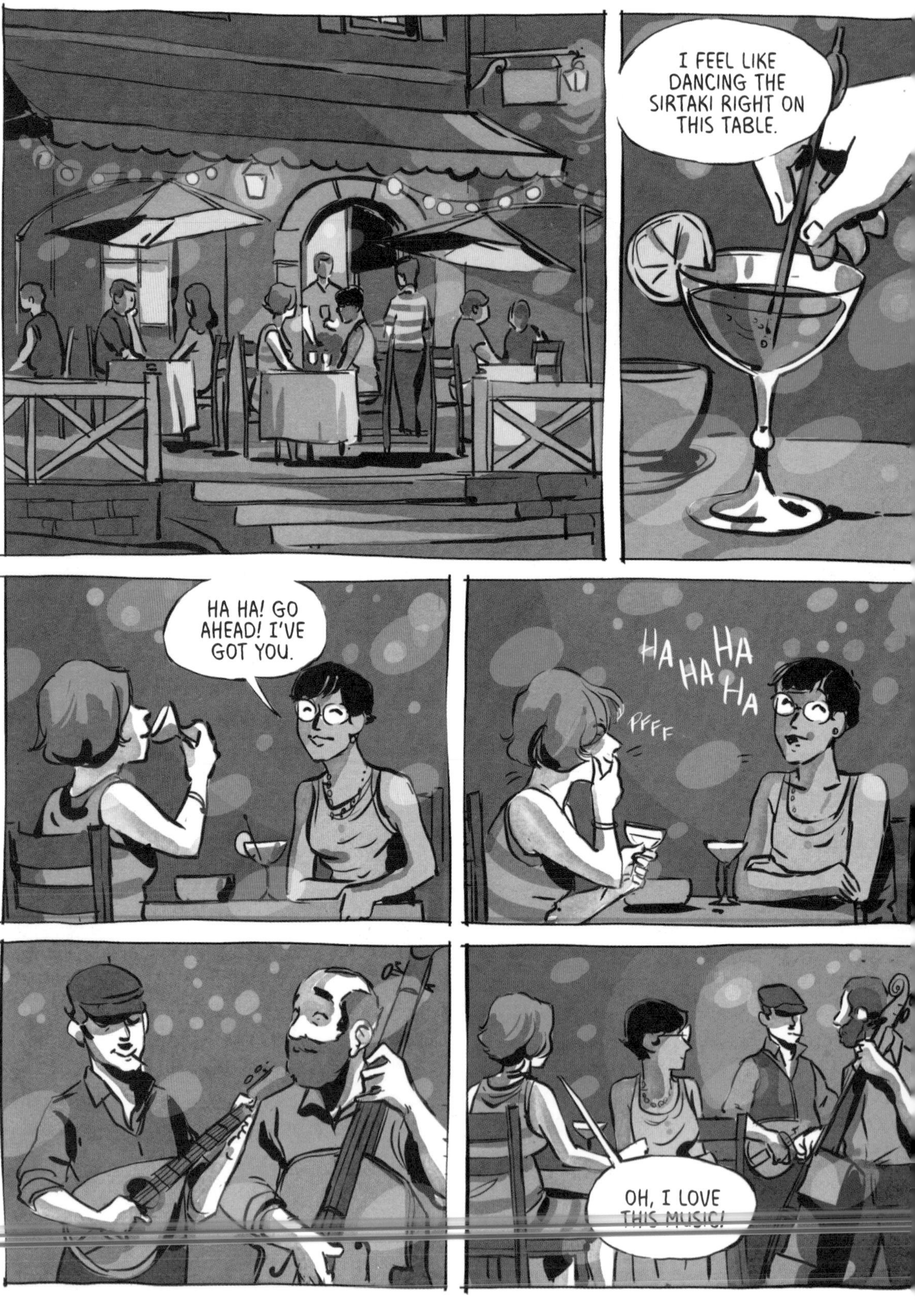
I FEEL LIKE DANCING THE SIRTAKI RIGHT ON THIS TABLE.
HA HA! GO AHEAD! I'VE GOT YOU.
HA HA HA HA HA
PFFF
OH, I LOVE THIS MUSIC!

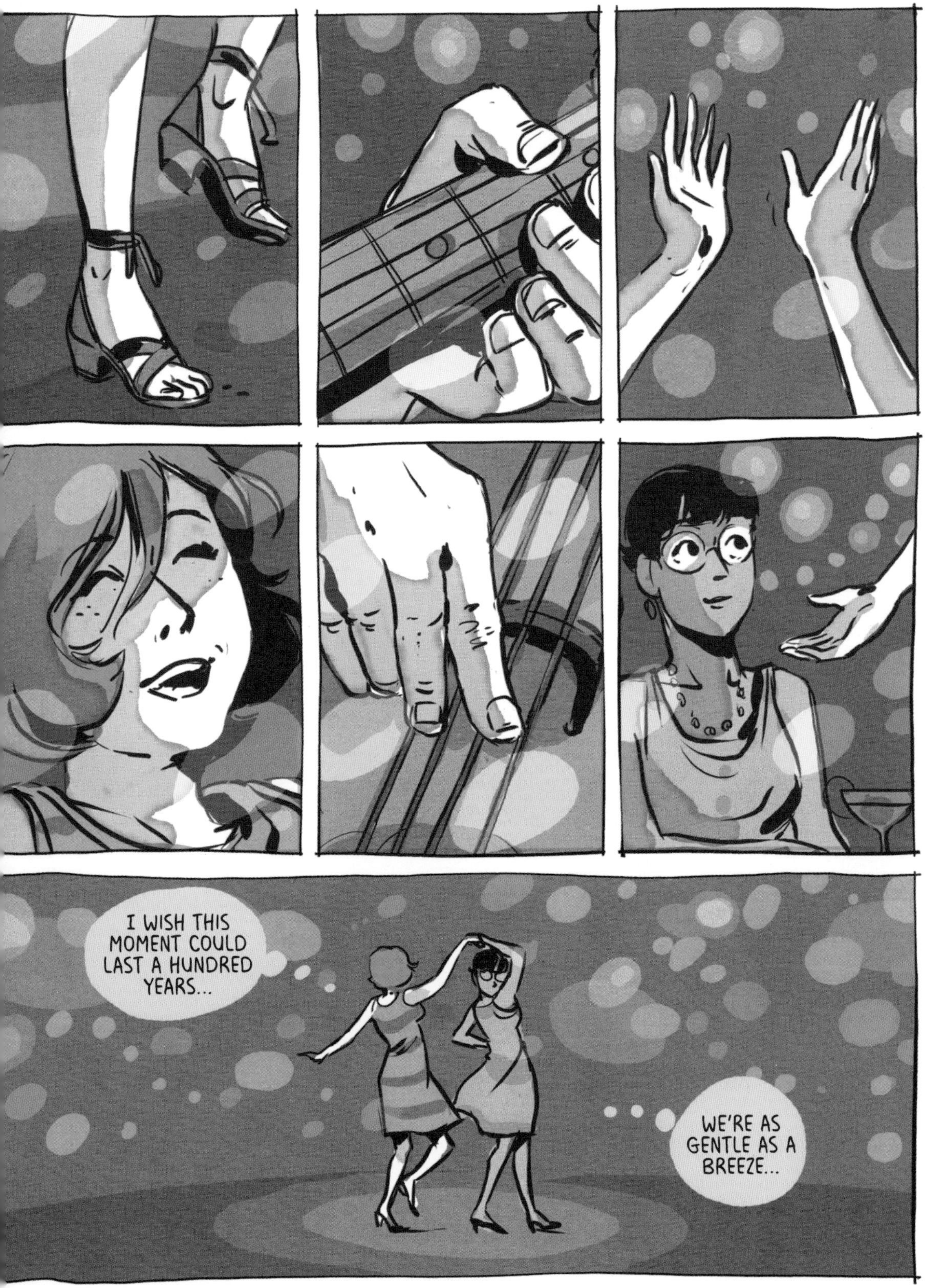
I WISH THIS MOMENT COULD LAST A HUNDRED YEARS...
WE'RE AS GENTLE AS A BREEZE...

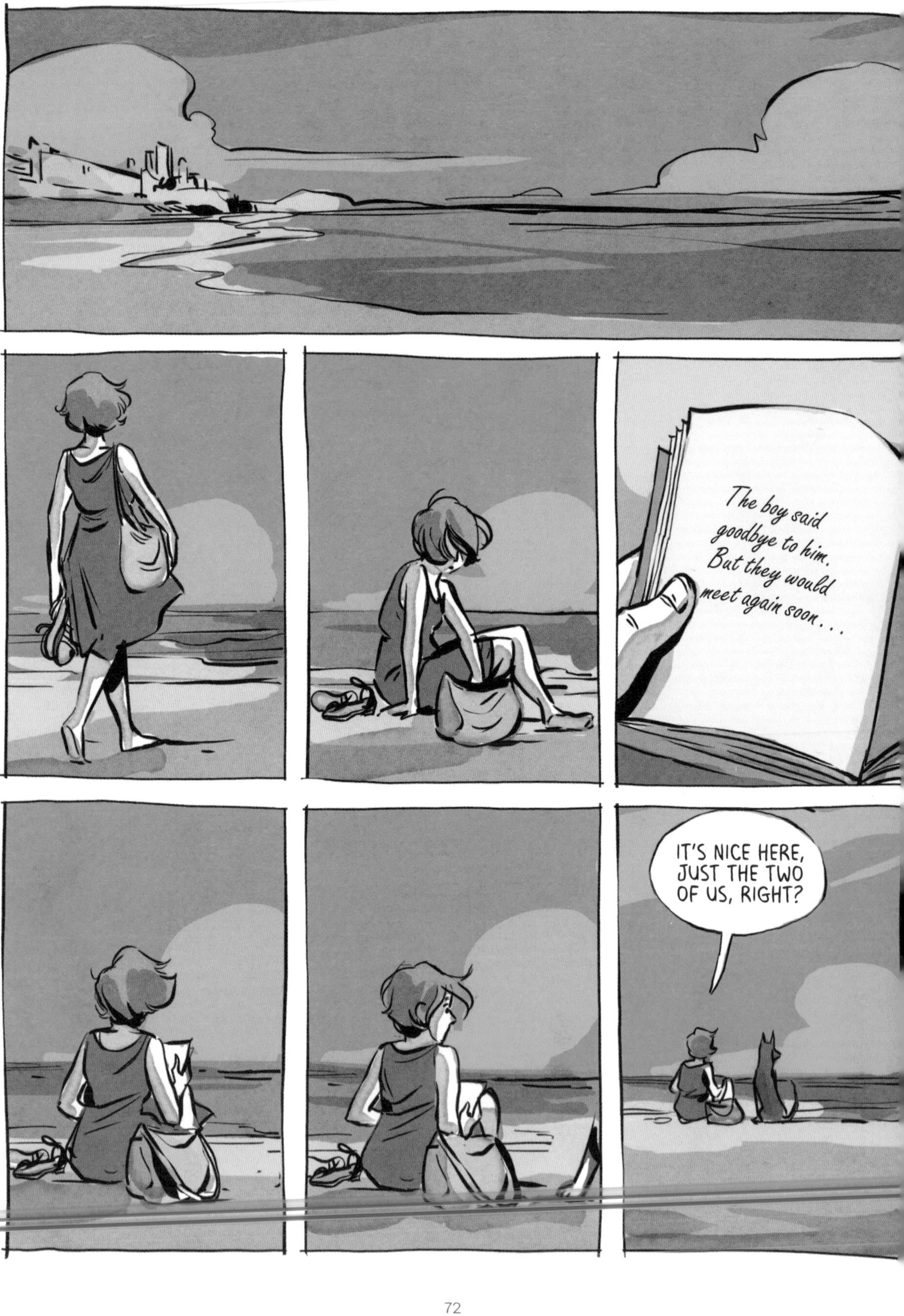
The boy said
goodbye to him.
But they would
meet again soon...
IT'S NICE HERE,
JUST THE TWO
OF US, RIGHT?

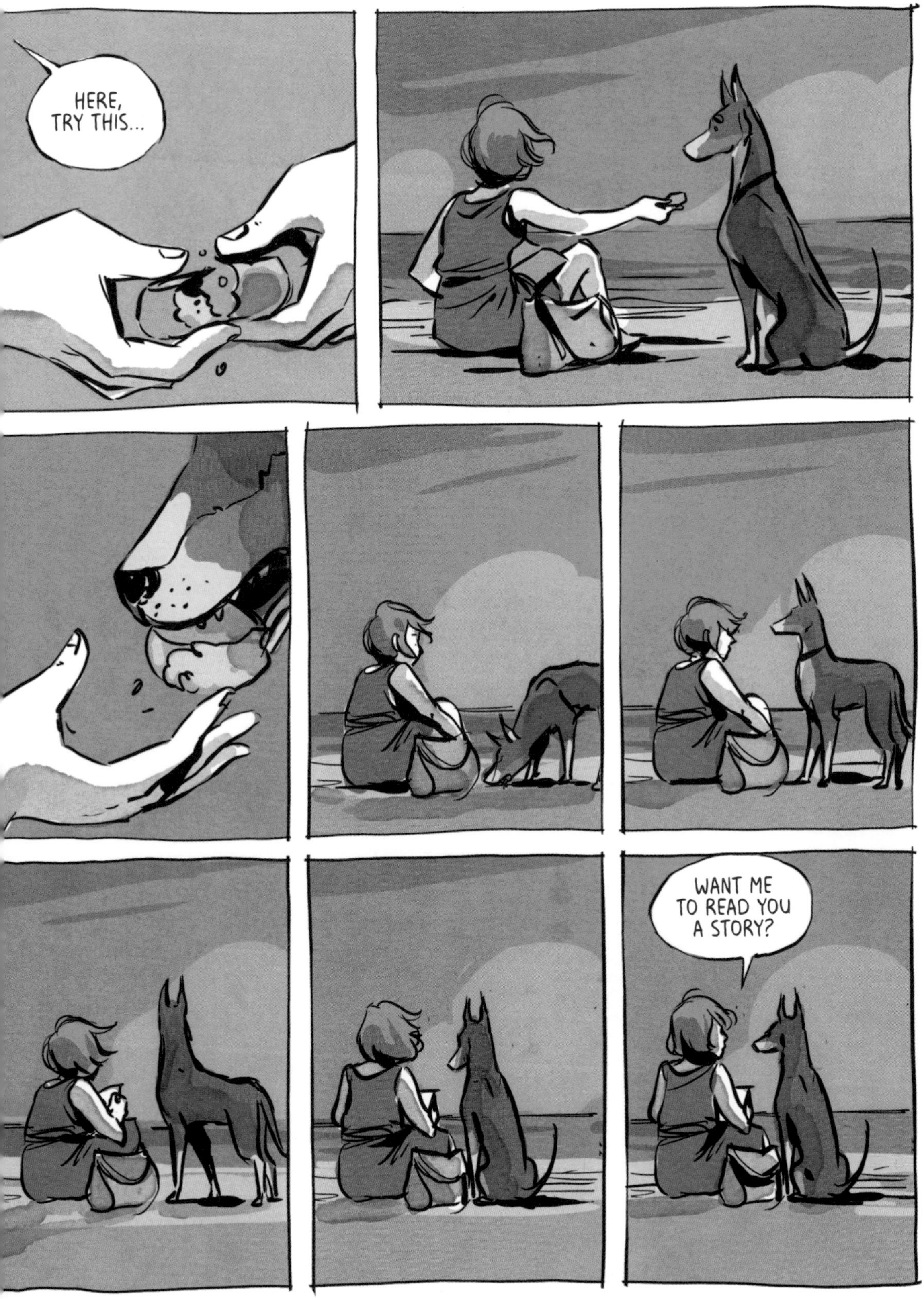
HERE, TRY THIS...
WANT ME TO READ YOU A STORY?

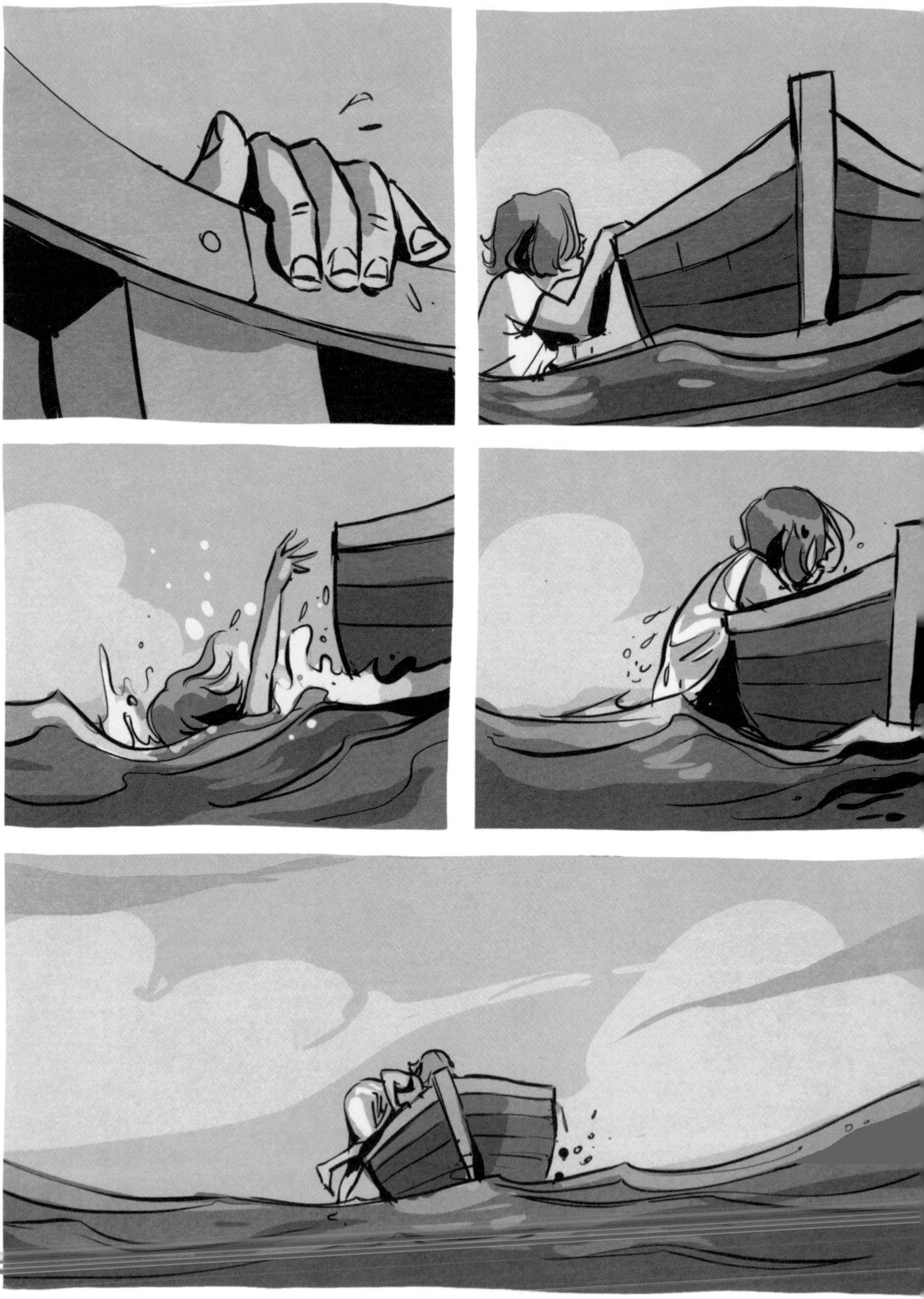

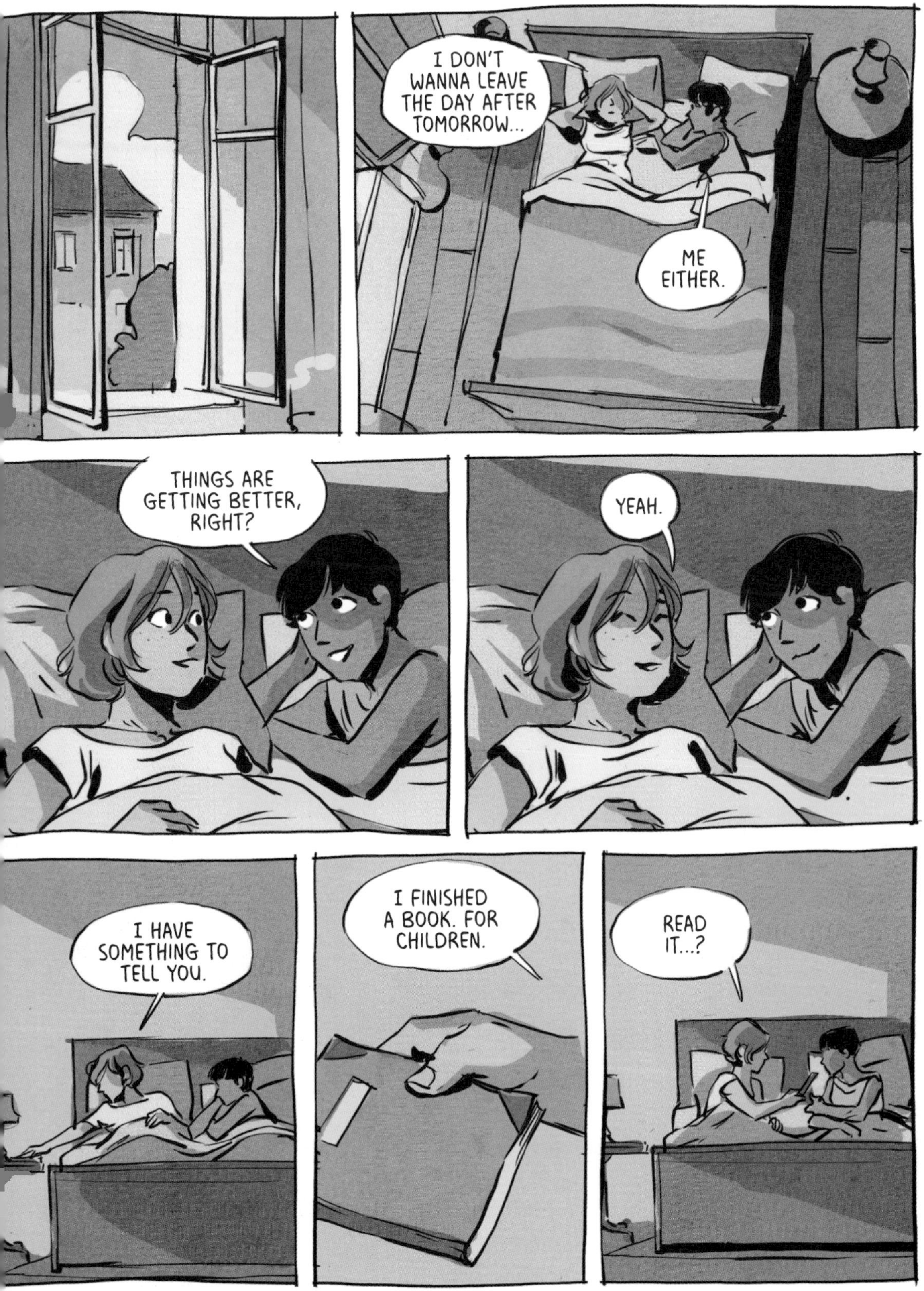
I DON'T WANNA LEAVE THE DAY AFTER TOMORROW...
ME EITHER.
THINGS ARE GETTING BETTER, RIGHT?
YEAH.
I HAVE SOMETHING TO TELL YOU.
I FINISHED A BOOK. FOR CHILDREN.
READ IT...?

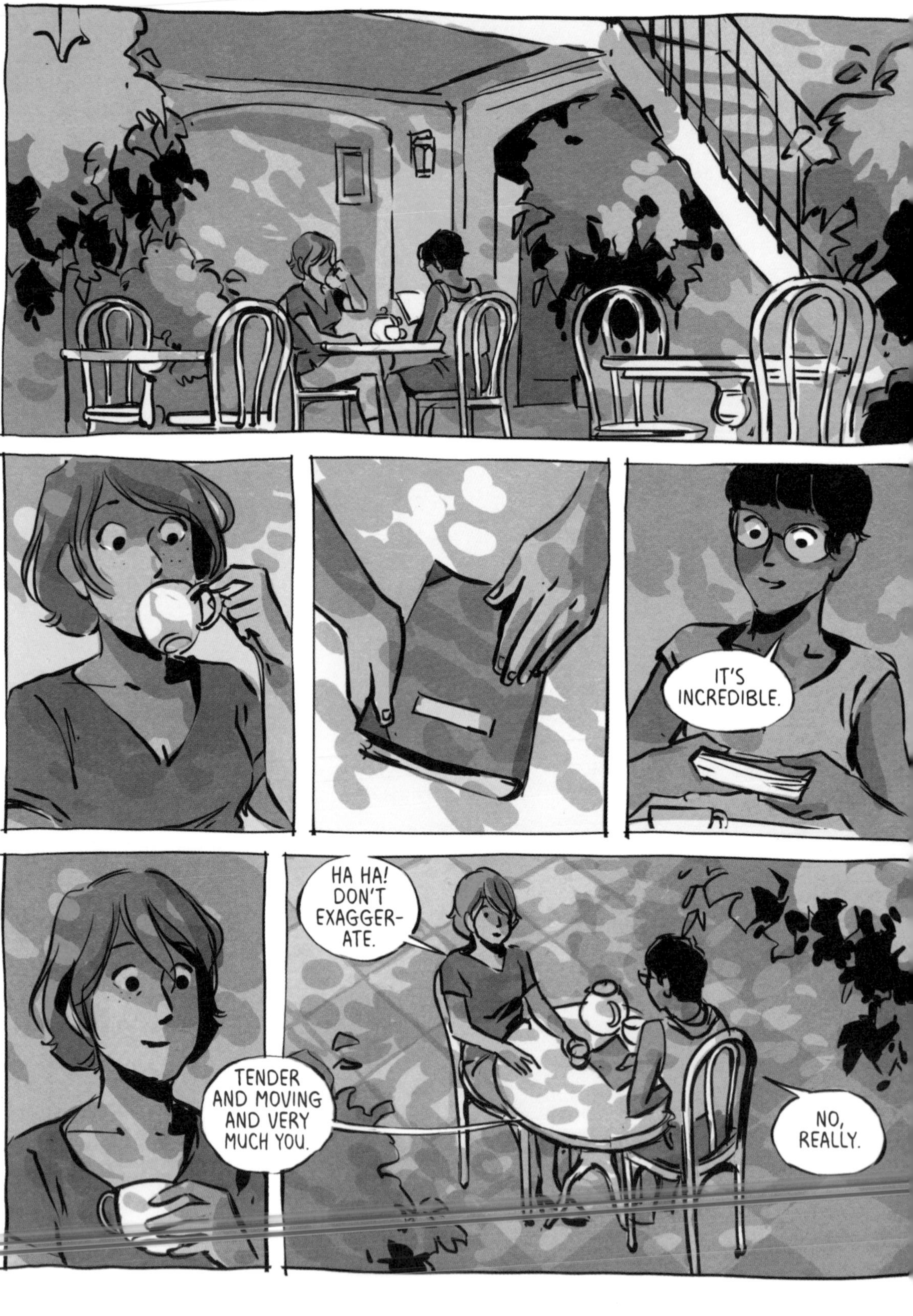
IT'S INCREDIBLE.
HA HA! DON'T EXAGGER-ATE.
TENDER AND MOVING AND VERY MUCH YOU.
NO, REALLY.

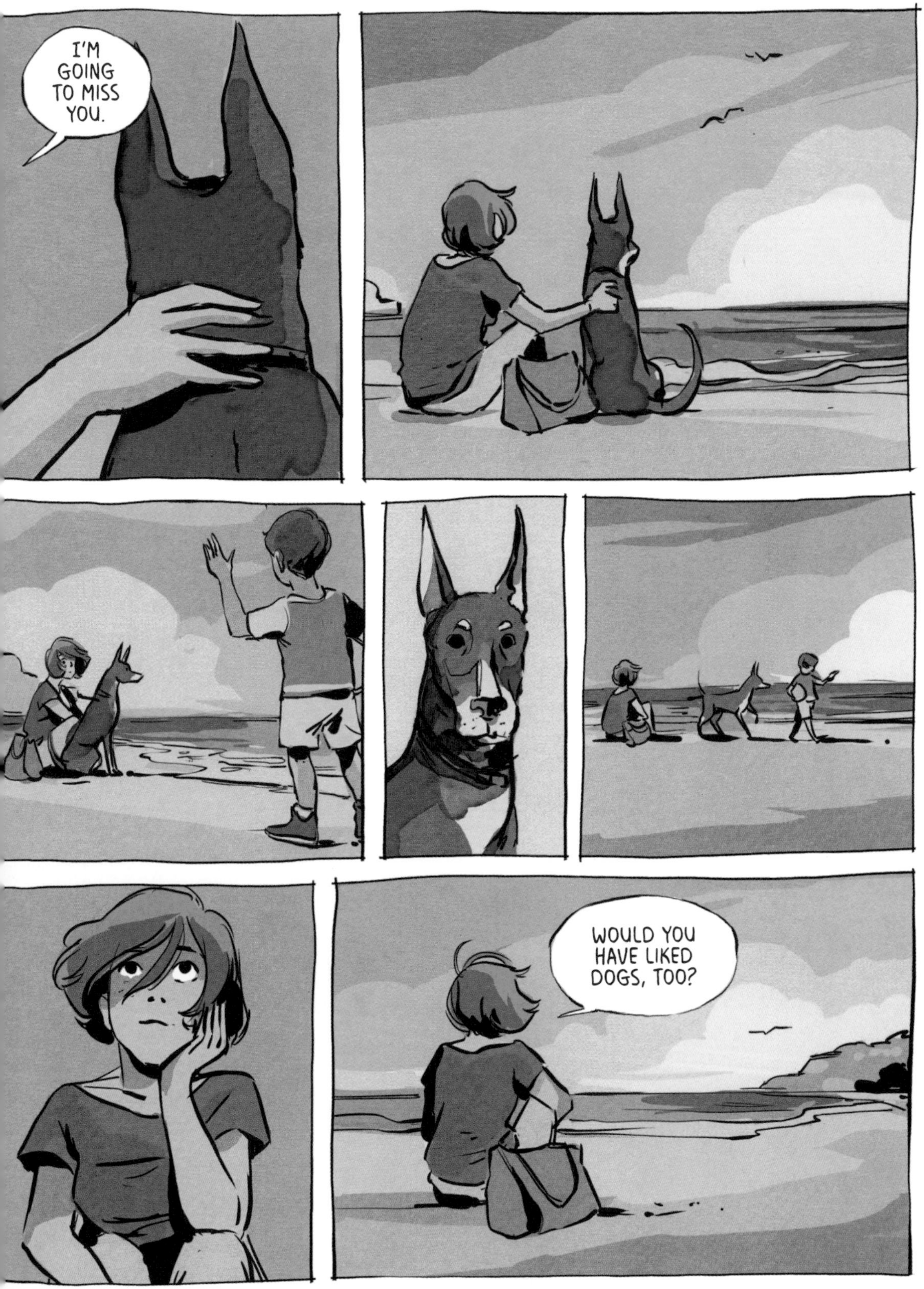
I'M GOING TO MISS YOU.
WOULD YOU HAVE LIKED DOGS, TOO?

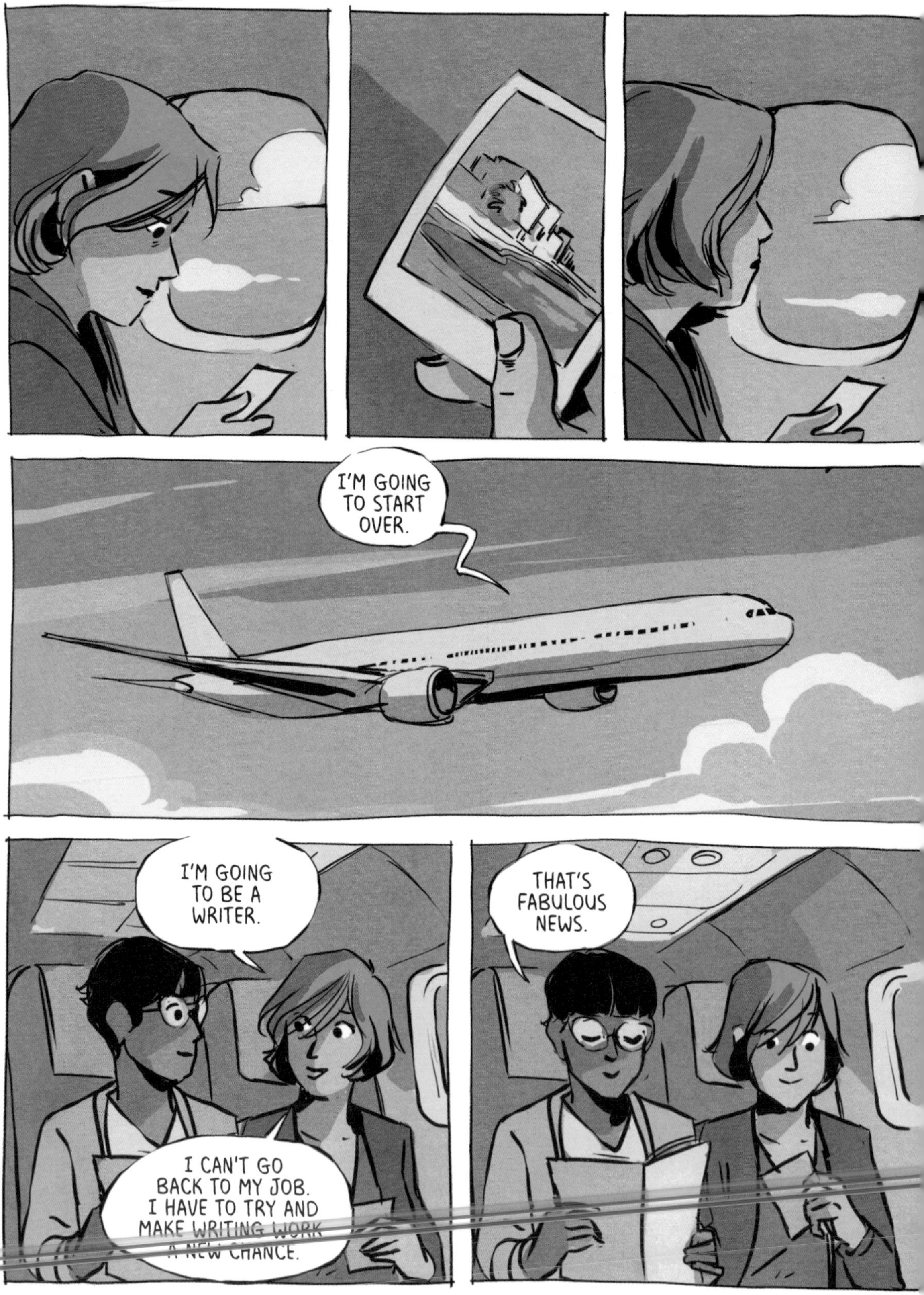
I'M GOING TO START OVER.
I'M GOING TO BE A WRITER.
I CAN'T GO BACK TO MY JOB. I HAVE TO TRY AND MAKE WRITING WORK A NEW CHANCE.
THAT'S FABULOUS NEWS.

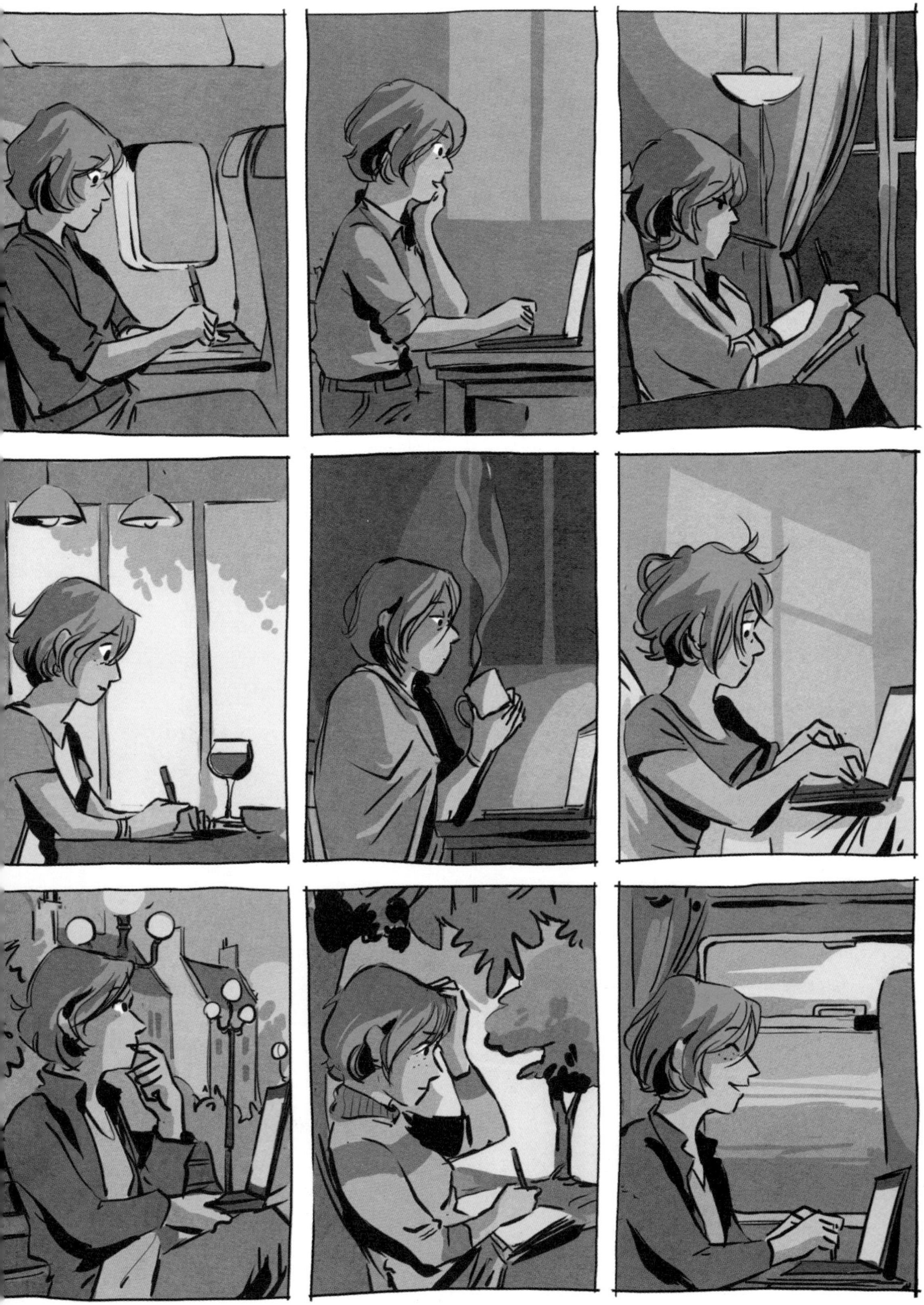

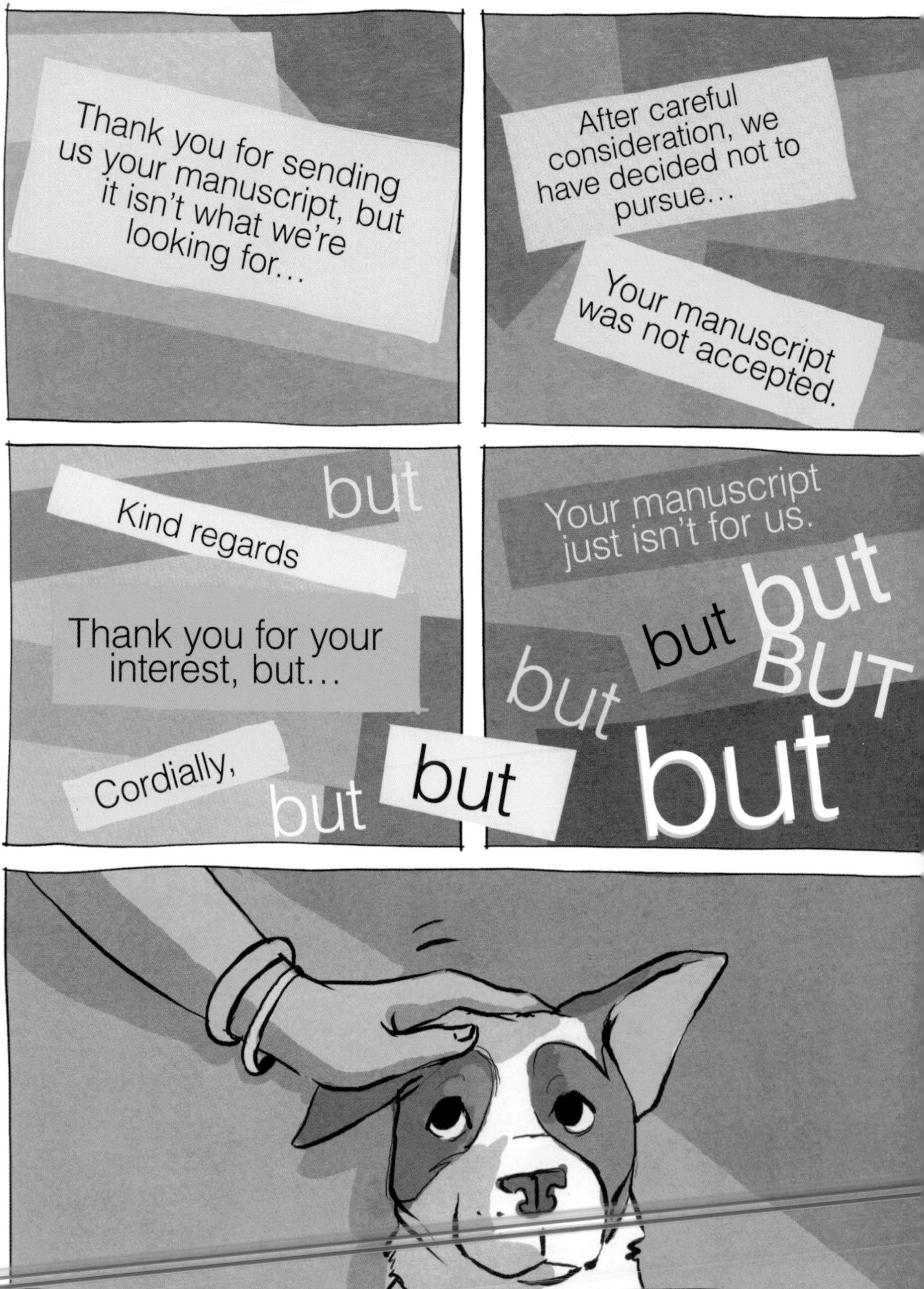

Thank you for sending us your manuscript, but it isn't what we're looking for...
After careful consideration, we have decided not to pursue...
Your manuscript was not accepted.
but
Kind regards
Thank you for your interest, but...
Cordially,
but
but
Your manuscript just isn't for us.
but
but
BUT
but
but

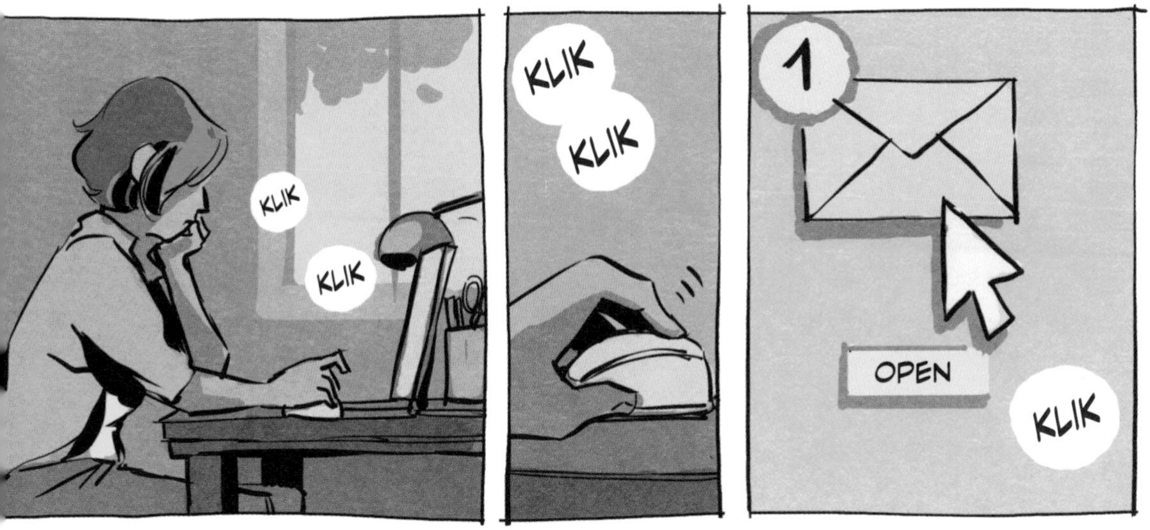
KLIK
KLIK
KLIK
KLIK
1
OPEN
KLIK

Dear Author,

We are very interested in your children's book and would like to publish it. Could we schedule a phone meeting to discuss it further?

Cordially,

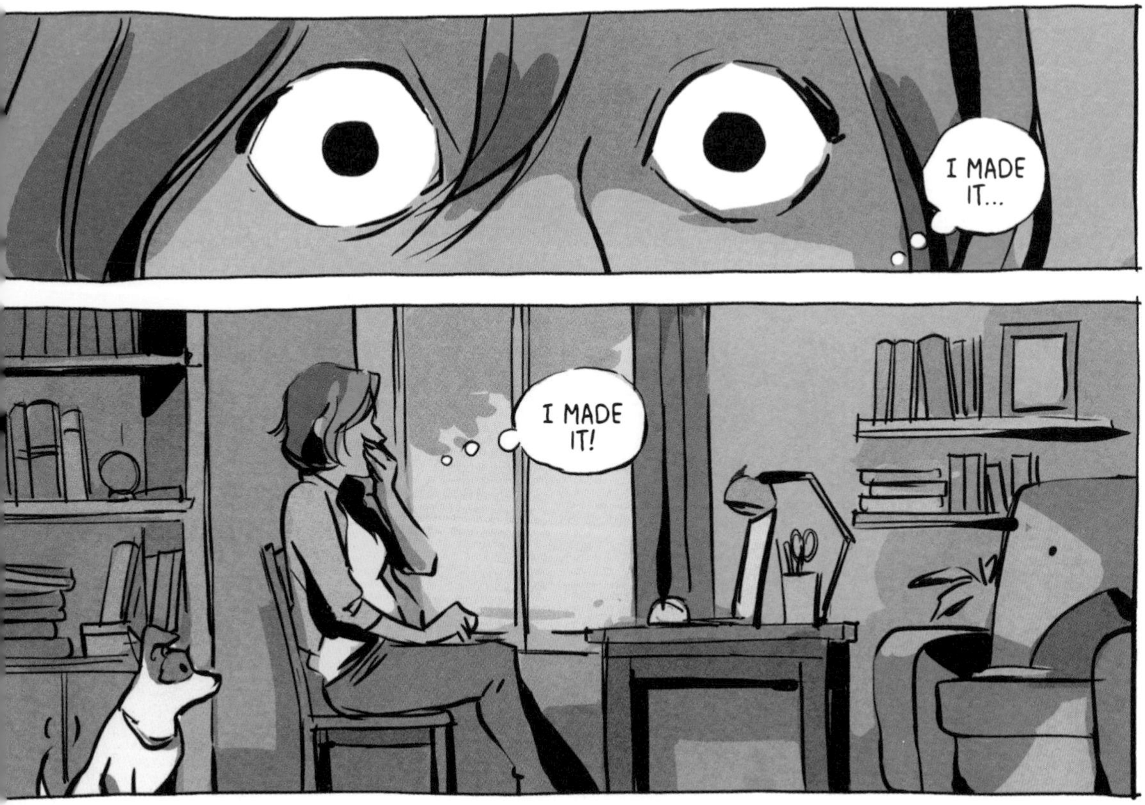
I MADE IT...
I MADE IT!

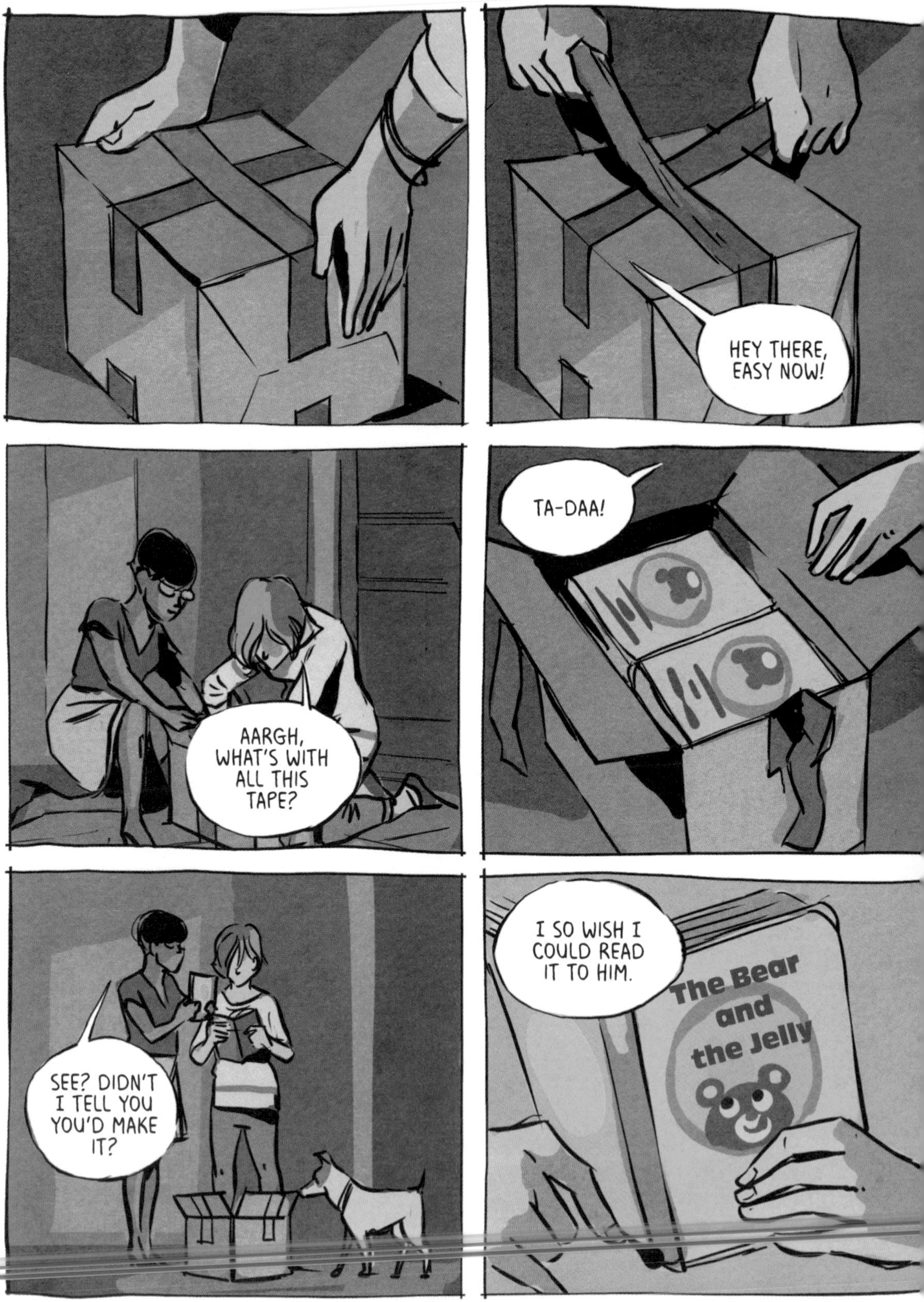
HEY THERE, EASY NOW!
AARGH, WHAT'S WITH ALL THIS TAPE?
TA-DAA!
SEE? DIDN'T I TELL YOU YOU'D MAKE IT?
I SO WISH I COULD READ IT TO HIM.
The Bear and the Jelly

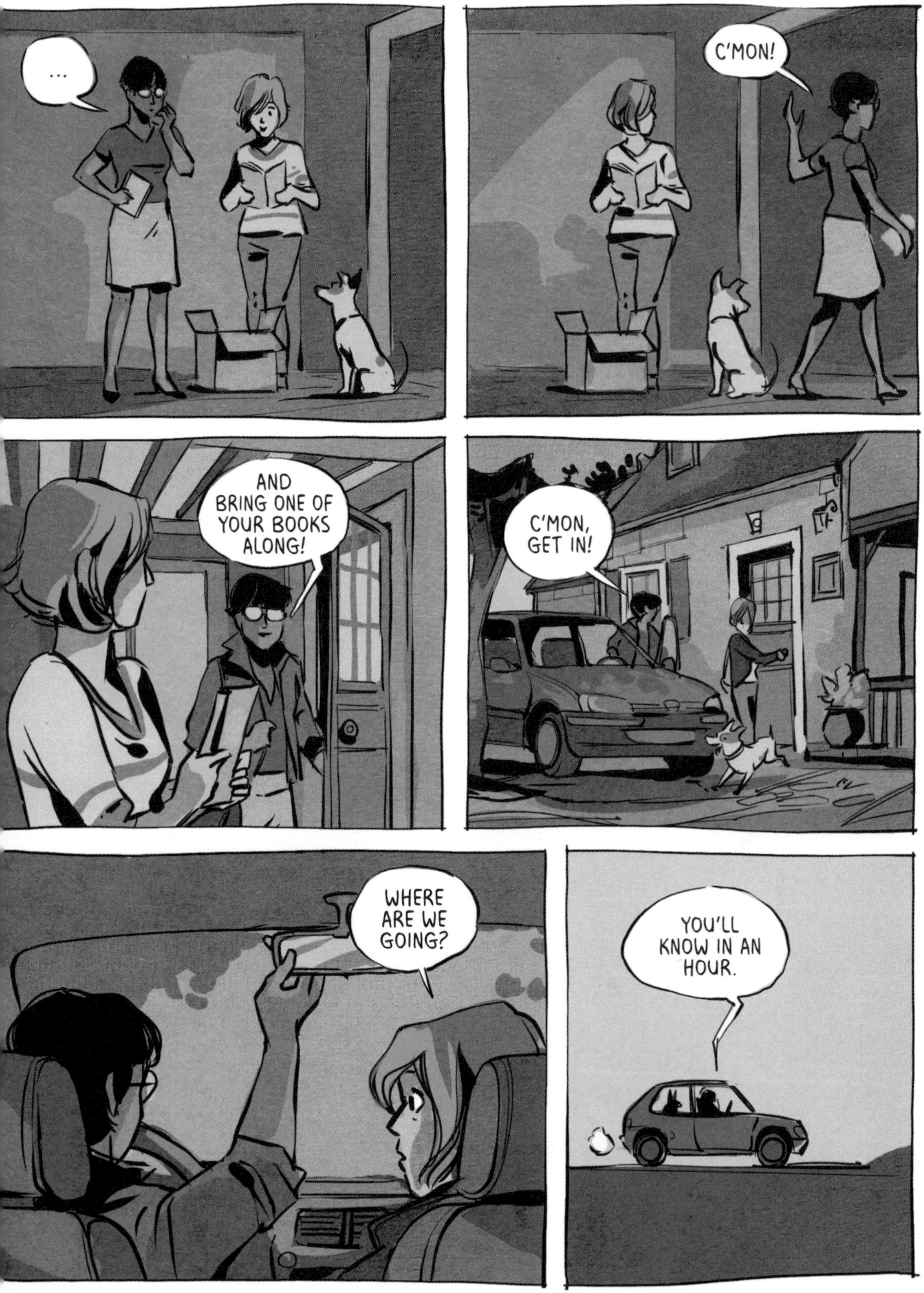
...
C'MON!
AND BRING ONE OF YOUR BOOKS ALONG!
C'MON, GET IN!
WHERE ARE WE GOING?
YOU'LL KNOW IN AN HOUR.

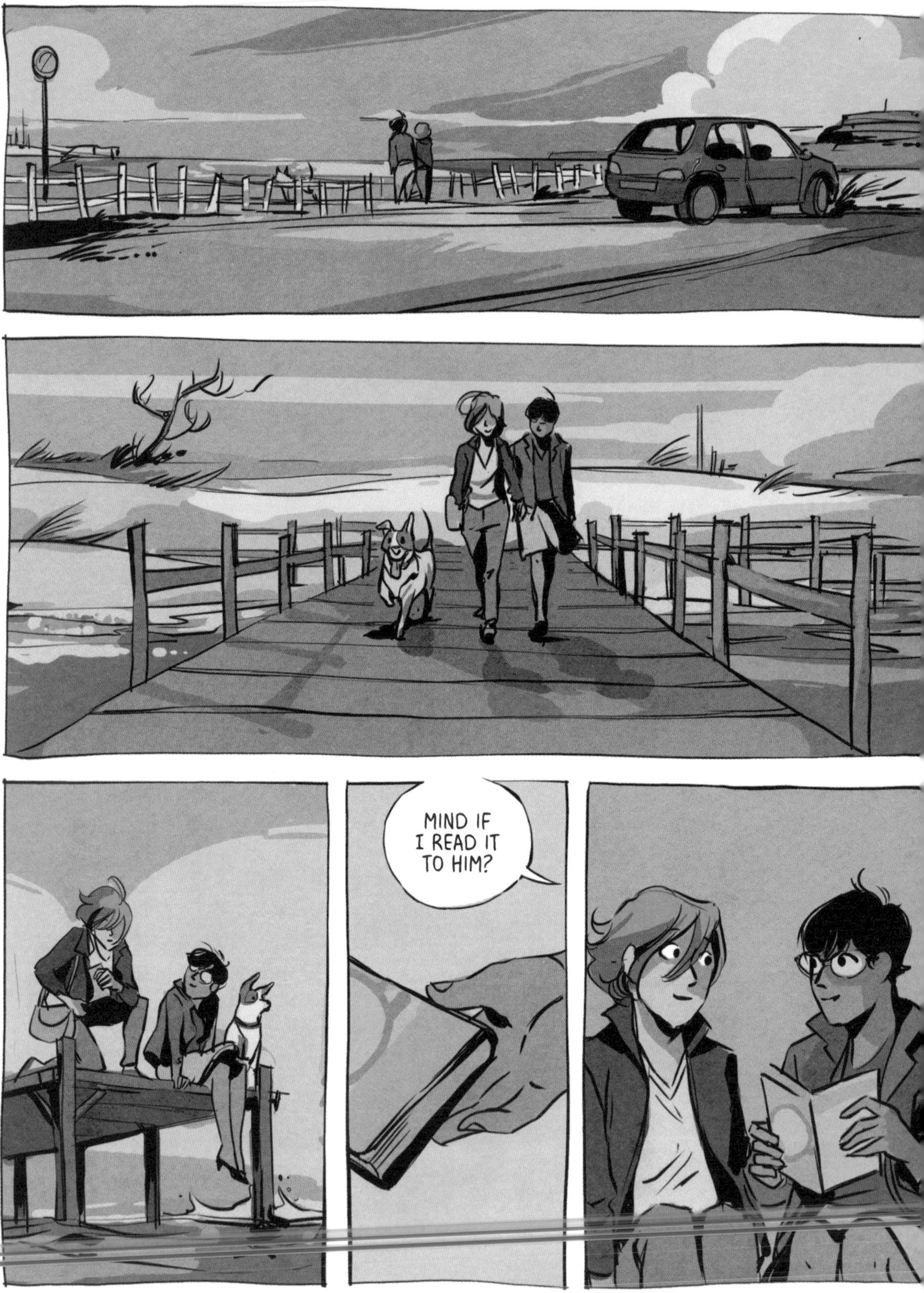
MIND IF
I READ IT
TO HIM?

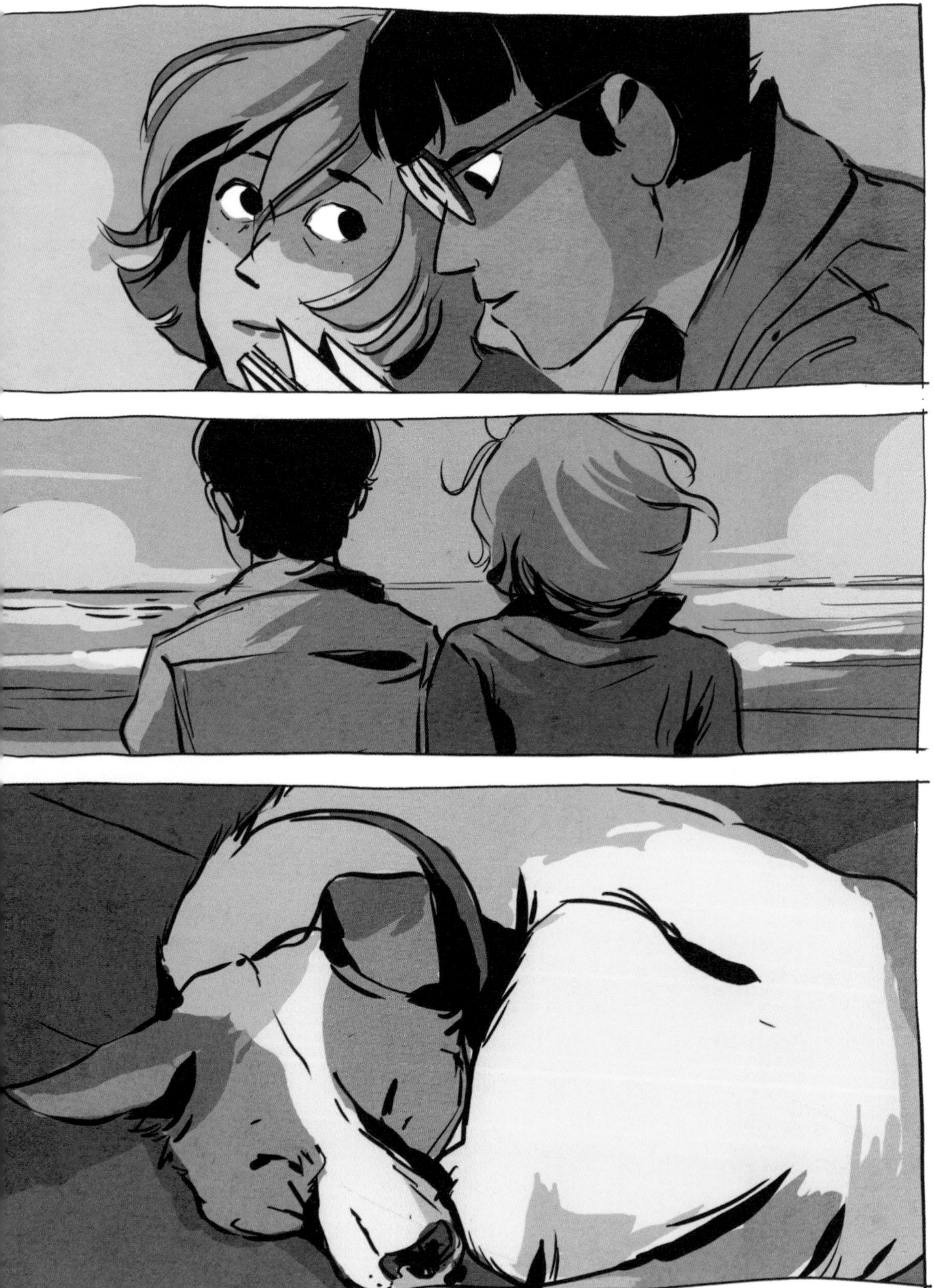

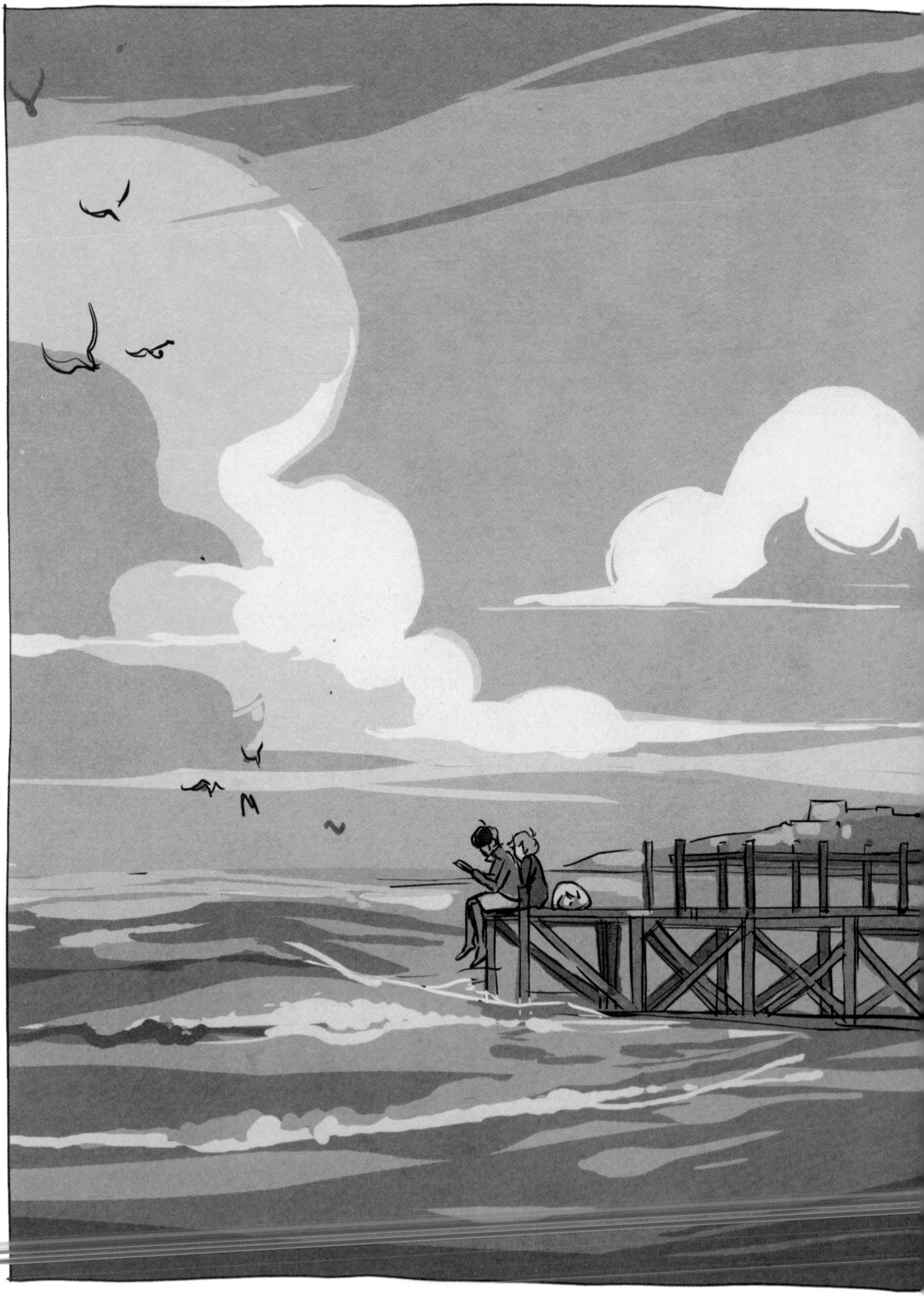

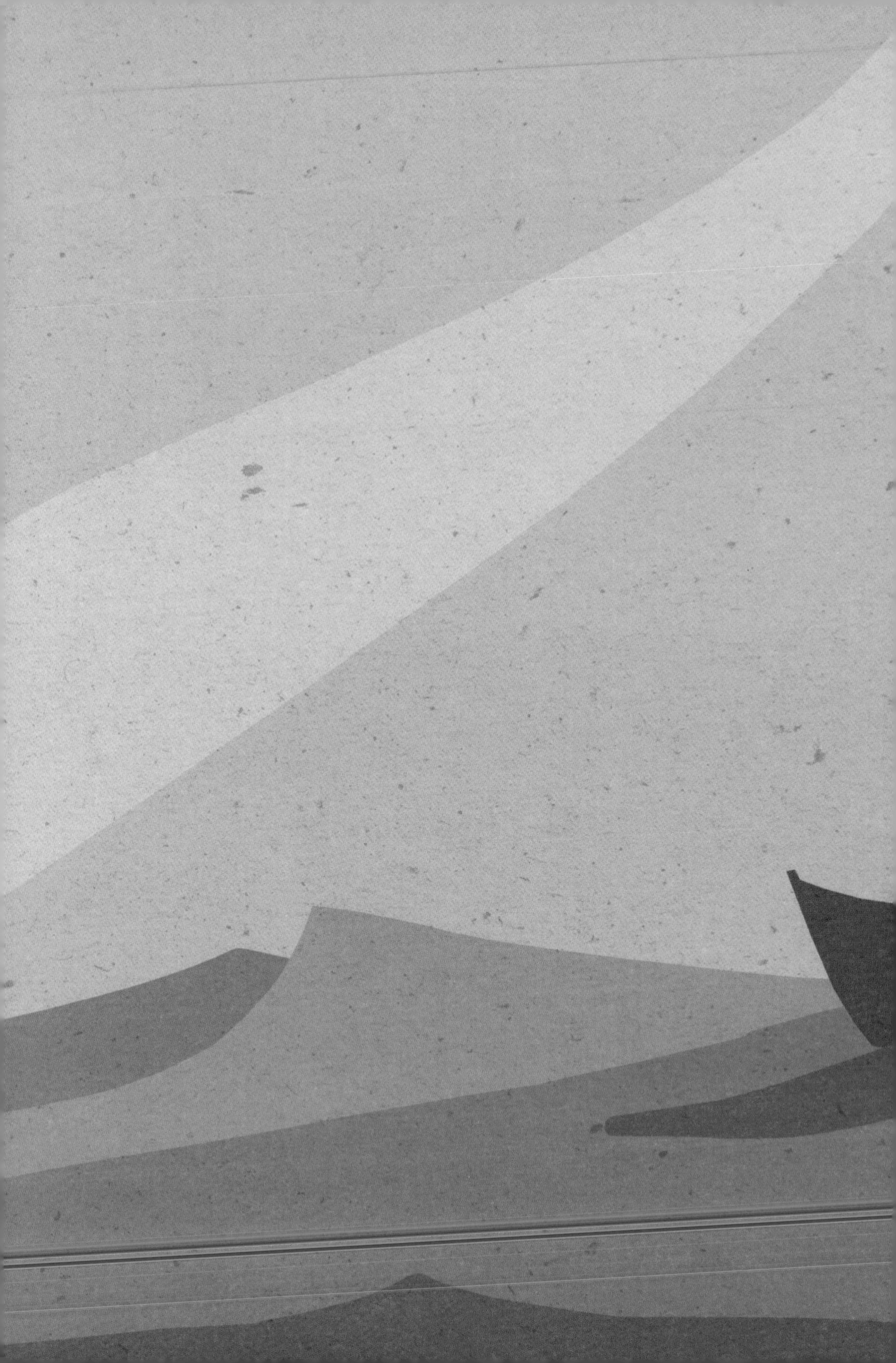

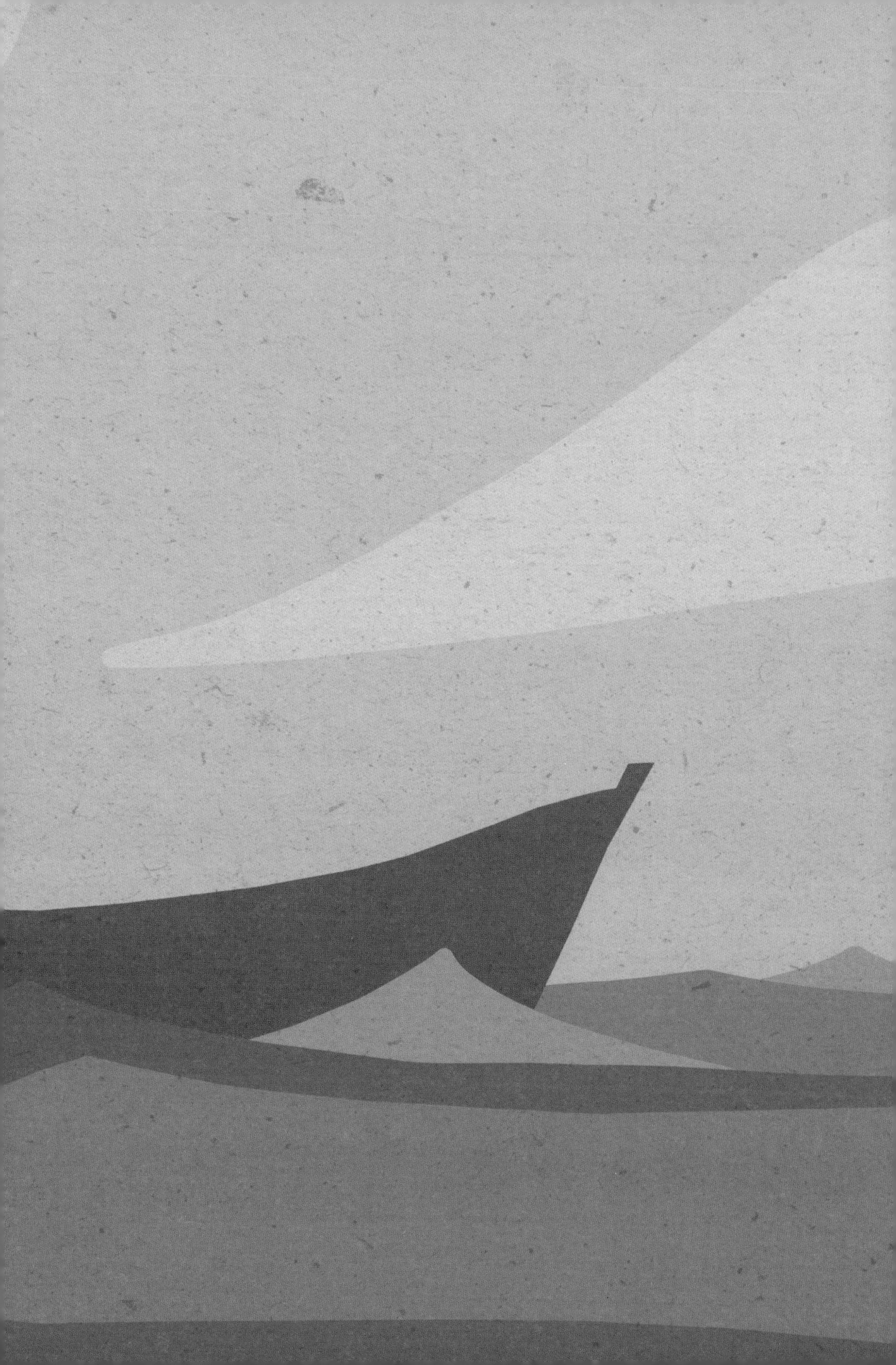

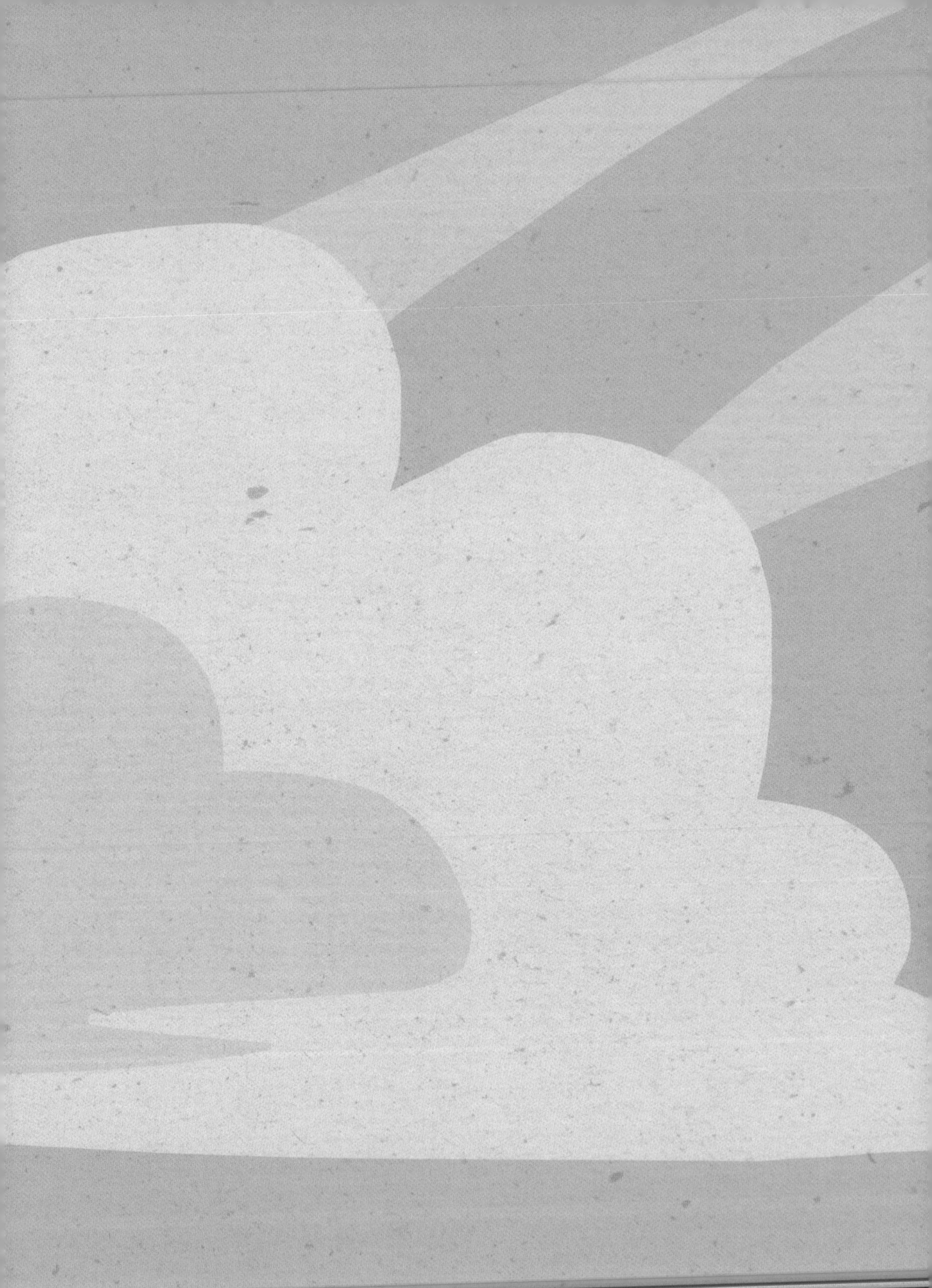

INGRID CHABBERT is the author of about sixty children's books and is currently growing a new readership through her first foray into graphic novels with *Waves* which is inspired by her personal story.

Artist **CAROLE MAUREL** first worked in animation before devoting herself to comics full-time. Her critically acclaimed graphic novel *Luisa: Now and Then* was released in 2018.

It happened in 2009.

After more than eight years together my partner and I thought we were preparing to share one of the most beautiful moments of our married life. It took me many years to finally manage to write about this painful event. However, I quickly knew that it would be necessary one day. I just had to wait. Wait to move forward through our mourning. Wait until tears and despair dried up. Wait until, little by little, life regained its rights. Wait, simply, to feel the strength to continue.

And when that was the case—when I found the strength—it would sink. I spent several days and nights there. I thought of all the couples who lived through this. I thought of all those who have experienced such a terrible loss, whatever it may be. Because I know that we all go through the same phases of both mourning and reconstruction.

I did not talk about the beginnings of our journey, however long and painful. I did not want this graphic novel to be immediately labeled as "yet another couple of women trying to have a baby".

It is above all an album about love, loss, reconstruction.

We cannot see him, but our son is still with us. A bit like a little star. I do not know if, without the strength he gave me, without the love and encouragement of my wife, I would have been able to get started as I did in writing and in this life of an author.

That's it, Waves, it's everything at once. And probably so many other things that, I hope, will speak to readers . . .

INGRID CHABBERT

DISCOVER VISIONARY CREATORS

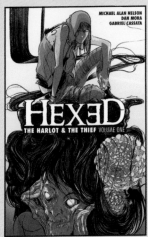

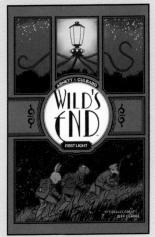

James Tynion IV
The Woods
Volume 1
ISBN: 978-1-60886-454-6 | $9.99 US
Volume 2
ISBN: 978-1-60886-495-9 | $14.99 US
Volume 3
ISBN: 978-1-60886-773-8 | $14.99 US

The Backstagers
Volume 1
ISBN: 978-1-60886-993-0 | $14.99 US

Simon Spurrier
Six-Gun Gorilla
ISBN: 978-1-60886-390-7 | $19.99 US

The Spire
ISBN: 978-1-60886-913-8 | $29.99 US

Weavers
ISBN: 978-1-60886-963-3 | $19.99 US

Mark Waid
Irredeemable
Volume 1
ISBN: 978-1-93450-690-5 | $16.99 US
Volume 2
ISBN: 978-1-60886-000-5 | $16.99 US

Incorruptible
Volume 1
ISBN: 978-1-60886-015-9 | $16.99 US
Volume 2
ISBN: 978-1-60886-028-9 | $16.99 US

Strange Fruit
ISBN: 978-1-60886-872-8 | $24.99 US

Michael Alan Nelson
Hexed The Harlot & The Thief
Volume 1
ISBN: 978-1-60886-718-9 | $14.99 US
Volume 2
ISBN: 978-1-60886-816-2 | $14.99 US

Day Men
Volume 1
ISBN: 978-1-60886-393-8 | $9.99 US
Volume 2
ISBN: 978-1-60886-852-0 | $9.99 US

Dan Abnett
Wild's End
Volume 1: First Light
ISBN: 978-1-60886-735-6 | $19.99 US
Volume 2: The Enemy Within
ISBN: 978-1-60886-877-3 | $19.99 US

Hypernaturals
Volume 1
ISBN: 978-1-60886-298-6 | $16.99 US
Volume 2
ISBN: 978-1-60886-319-8 | $19.99 US

DISCOVER
GROUNDBREAKING TITLES

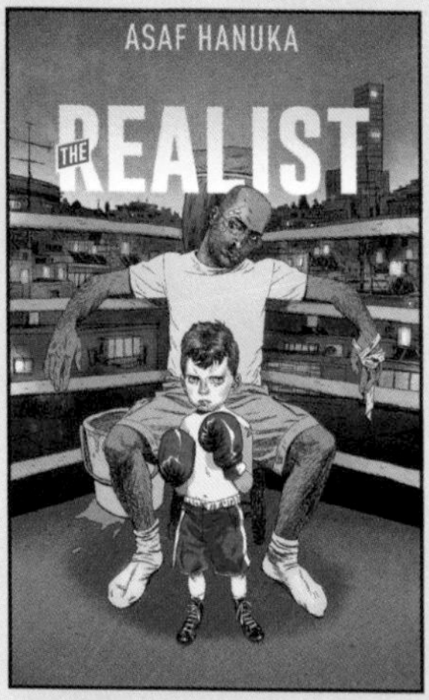
ASAF HANUKA
THE REALIST

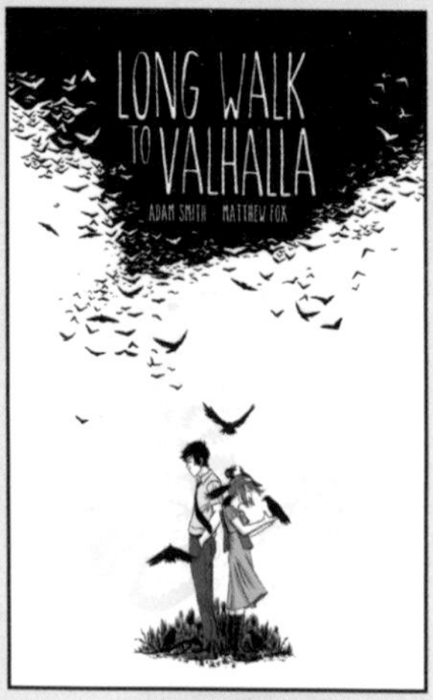
LONG WALK TO VALHALLA
ADAM SMITH · MATTHEW FOX

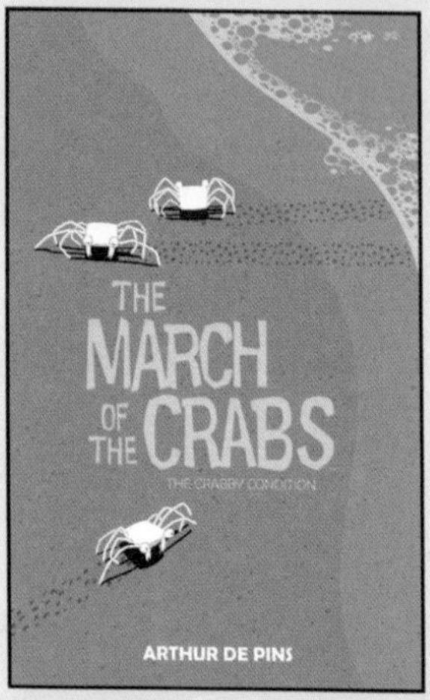
THE MARCH OF THE CRABS
THE CRABBY CONDITION
ARTHUR DE PINS

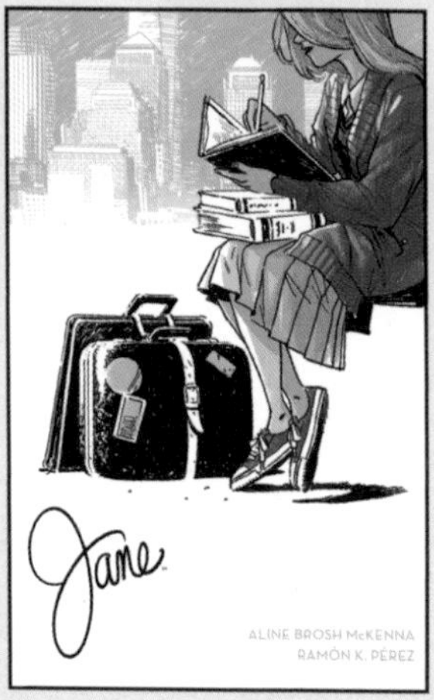
Jane
ALINE BROSH McKENNA
RAMÓN K. PÉREZ

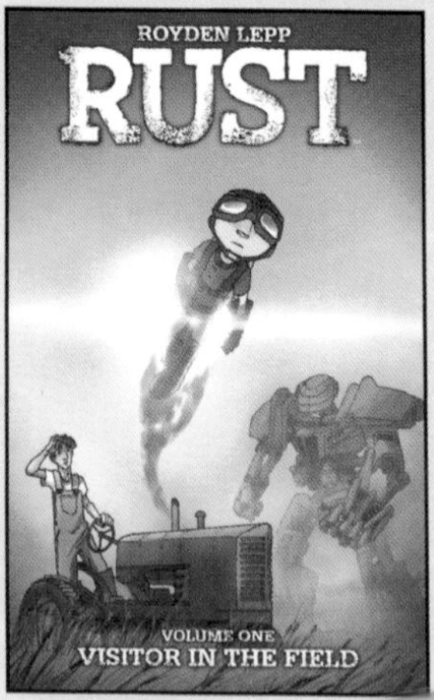
ROYDEN LEPP
RUST
VOLUME ONE
VISITOR IN THE FIELD

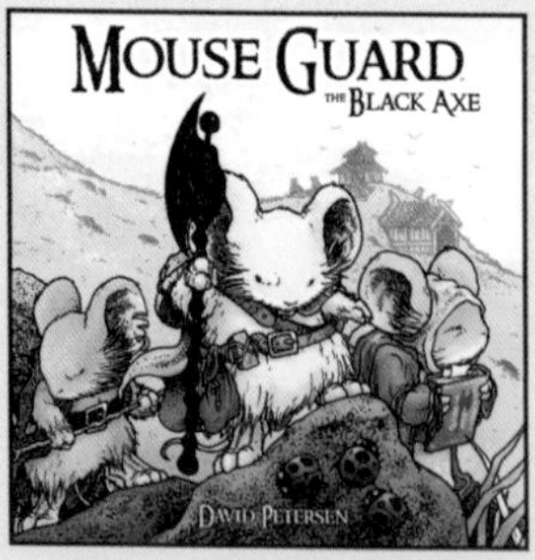
MOUSE GUARD
THE BLACK AXE
DAVID PETERSEN

The Realist
Asaf Hanuka
ISBN: 978-1-60886-688-5 | $24.99 US

The Realist: Plug and Play
Asaf Hanuka
ISBN: 978-1-60886-953-4 | $24.99 US

Long Walk to Valhalla
Adam Smith, Matt Fox
ISBN: 978-1-60886-692-2 | $24.99 US

The March of The Crabs
Arthur De Pins
Volume 1: The Crabby Condition
ISBN: 978-1-60886-689-2 | $19.99 US
Volume 2: The Empire of the Crabs
ISBN: 978-1-68415-014-4 | $19.99 US

Jane
Aline Brosh McKenna, Ramón K. Pérez
ISBN: 978-1-60886-981-7 | $24.99 US

Rust
Royden Lepp
Volume 0: The Boy Soldier
ISBN: 978-1-60886-806-3 | $10.99 US
Volume 1: Visitor in the Field
ISBN: 978-1-60886-894-0 | $14.99 US
Volume 2: Secrets of the Cell
ISBN: 978-1-60886-895-7 | $14.99 US

Mouse Guard
David Petersen
Mouse Guard: Fall 1152
ISBN: 978-1-93238-657-8 | $24.95 US
Mouse Guard: Winter 1152
ISBN: 978-1-93238-674-5 | $24.95 US
Mouse Guard: The Black Axe
ISBN: 978-1-93639-306-0 | $24.95 US

The Cloud
K.I. Zachopoulos, Vincenzo Balzano
ISBN: 978-1-60886-725-7 | $24.99 US

Cursed Pirate Girl Coloring Book
Jeremy A. Bastian
ISBN: 978-1-60886-947-3 | $16.99 US

ARCHAIA

AVAILABLE AT YOUR LOCAL COMICS SHOP AND BOOKSTORE
WWW.**BOOM-STUDIOS**.COM